The
WORST-CASE SCENARIO
Survival Handbook:
HOLIDAYS

The
WORST-CASE SCENARIO
Survival Handbook:
HOLIDAYS

By Joshua Piven and David Borgenicht
Illustrations by Brenda Brown

CHRONICLE BOOKS

SAN FRANCISCO

Library of Congress Cataloging-in-Publication Data available.

ISBN: 0-8118-3599-5

Manufactured in the United States of America

Typeset in Adobe Caslon, Bundesbahn Pi, and Zapf Dingbats

Designed by Terry Peterson

A **QUIRK** Book
www.quirkproductions.com
Visit www.worstcasescenarios.com

Distributed in Canada by Raincoast Books
9050 Shaughnessy Street
Vancouver, BC V6P 6E5
10 9 8 7 6 5 4 3 2 1

Chronicle Books LLC
85 Second Street
San Francisco, California 94105
www.chroniclebooks.com

WARNING

When a life is imperiled or a dire situation is at hand, safe alternatives may not exist—and elves are not always around to help out. To deal with the holiday worst-case scenarios presented in this book, we highly recommend—insist, actually—that the best course of action is to consult a professionally trained expert. But because highly trained professionals may not always be available when the safety or sanity of individuals is at risk, we have asked experts on various subjects to describe the techniques they might employ in these seasonal emergency situations. The publisher, authors, and experts disclaim any liability from any injury that may result from the use, proper or improper, of the information contained in this book. All the information in this book comes directly from experts, but we do not guarantee that the information contained herein is complete, safe, or accurate, nor should it be considered a substitute for your good judgment, your common sense, or your sense of peace on earth and goodwill toward men. And finally, nothing in this book should be construed or interpreted to infringe on the rights or presents of other persons or to violate criminal statutes; we urge you to obey all laws and respect all rights, including property rights, of others.

—The Authors

CONTENTS

You better watch out . . .
—"Santa Claus Is Coming to Town"

INTRODUCTION

The world thinks of the Holidays as a time of peace and joy—a time when all is harmonious, and we all join together eating, drinking, and generally being merry. We give gifts, we donate to charities, we spend time with our friends and loved ones—what could possibly go wrong?

Consider this: More suicides, car accidents, family arguments, and food and alcohol poisonings take place during the months of November and December than any other time of the year. Add travel mishaps, kitchen disasters, snow- and ice-related injuries, electrocutions, tree-trimming catastrophes, and gift-related traumas—there's no such thing as a silent night when it comes to the holidays.

You may not be able to control Mother Nature, acts of God, mischievous elves, or bad cooks. But you can plan ahead to make sure that you're ready to act when your holiday plans take an unscheduled dive.

We sincerely hope that the worst that awaits you this holiday season is merely a minor mishap—a slightly overcooked turkey, a precariously balanced Christmas tree, or an unwanted gift. But in case tidings somewhat less comforting and joyful come your way, we want you to be prepared.

And so, as we did with our other *Worst-Case Scenario Survival Handbooks*, we've consulted dozens of highly trained professionals to come up with clear, step-by-step instructions for how to survive the perils of cooking and entertaining, friends and family, shopping, and assorted emergencies indoors and in the great outdoors. We spoke with chimney sweeps, physics professors, wilderness survival instructors, travel journalists, neurologists, craftmakers, professional carolers, gift consultants, motivational speakers, veterinarians, dentists, etiquette instructors, and dozens of others to obtain the responses to the worst worst-case scenarios we could imagine.

From how to extinguish a grease fire to how to fend off a charging reindeer, from how to deal with a runaway parade balloon to how to safely fall from a ladder, and from how to repurpose a fruitcake to how to make an emergency menorah, this handy guide should keep you safe and sound—at least between the end of November and New Year's Day. In a useful appendix, we've also included a New Year's Resolution-O-Matic and a sample "There is no Santa Claus" speech.

Being prepared is the best present you can give others—or yourself. (This book will fit in every stocking and under every tree.) With this guide in hand, you will be all set. So relax and enjoy the holidays. We hope that all your wishes come true and that your scenarios are best-case scenarios. But don't count on it.

—**The Authors**

CHAPTER 1

COOKING AND ENTERTAINING

HOW TO EXTINGUISH A BURNING TURKEY

1 Close the oven and broiler doors.
Turn the oven off.

2 Open nearby windows.
Smoke will pour out of the oven vent. Turn the vent-fan in the hood above the stove to its highest setting and open windows to help clear smoke. If possible, close the doors to the kitchen to contain the smoke. If you cannot close off the kitchen, open as many other windows in the building as possible to establish cross-ventilation.

Close the oven door immediately if the turkey is on fire.

3 | **Wait five minutes.**
Ovens are designed for high heat, so it should contain the fire without a problem. Keep the oven door closed to avoid adding oxygen to the fire.

4 | **Open the oven door slightly.**
Keep your face well back from the oven when you open the door. After five minutes, the turkey fire should have burned itself out. If it is still burning, close the door immediately and wait several minutes before opening it again. If the fire continues to burn for more than 10 minutes, call the fire department.

5 | **Remove the burned bird.**
Use caution: It will be extremely hot. Place the bird on a cutting board or platter. Wait at least 10 minutes before touching the turkey or attempting to rescue the meat. Often only the skin and fat will be burned. (See "How to Serve Burnt Turkey," page 18.)

Be Aware

- Oven fires can usually be extinguished without help from the fire department. However, oven seals may fail in a high-heat fire, causing the fire to spread to surrounding areas. Have someone standing by the phone to call for help if needed.
- Do not attempt to pull a flaming turkey out of the oven: You risk grease burns on your arms and face.
- Do not attempt to smother a flaming turkey while it is in the oven. The high temperatures and flaming grease may ignite the material.

- Do not attempt to douse the fire by throwing flour, baking soda, gravy, or any other products on a flaming turkey. These may be combustible and may cause grease to spatter. Using a fire extinguisher will render the bird inedible.

How to Serve Burnt Turkey

1 Remove the skin and charred sections.
Discard these burned parts.

2 Slice the turkey.

3 Pick out the scorched pieces.
Usually the burned portion will be white (breast) meat, which has less fat. Discard it.

4 Check the dark meat.
Some dark meat may also be severely overcooked. Pick out the moist sections and put them on a platter that has been warmed in the oven. Cover and set aside.

5 Moisten dry dark meat.
Layer the salvaged but dry dark meat in a roasting pan. Soak it with several cups of chicken broth and melted butter. Cover it with a cloth and put it in a warm oven (make sure the oven is turned off). Let the meat rest for a few minutes. Drain and remove meat from pan and place on serving tray. Do not use a microwave to warm the meat or the meat will toughen.

6 | Fatten the gravy.
Add one stick of butter to a boiling pot of gravy, let the butter melt, and allow the gravy to cool to serving temperature. Pour the mixture over the turkey after it has been carved.

7 | Make turkey hash.
If all else fails, chop the meat, toss with potatoes and bacon, and offer your guests turkey hash. Tell them it's an old family tradition. Serve with large glasses of water.

HOW TO PREVENT A TURKEY FROM EXPLODING

1 | Use a maximum of four beaten eggs in the stuffing.
Eggs expand as they cook and can force stuffing to explode out of the turkey's abdomen.

2 | Stuff the bird loosely.
Leave several inches of space for the stuffing to expand as it roasts.

3 | Keep a close watch on the bird as it cooks.
Check the turkey every 20 minutes or so. If the stuffing begins to leak out of the abdominal cavity, remove several spoonfuls.

Be Aware
Cooking the stuffing separately avoids potential bacterial contamination of the stuffing from the turkey and will also avoid any possibility of explosion.

How to Keep a Turkey Moist During Cooking

⭐ **Soak the bird overnight in brine.**
To make brine, dissolve one pound of salt per gallon of water; it should be as salty as seawater. Put the mixture in a large bucket (use plastic to avoid any metallic taste). Cover and leave the bird outside to keep it cool. If the temperature is above 50° F or well below 32° F, keep it refrigerated instead.

⭐ **Remove the legs of the turkey before cooking it.**
Dark meat takes longer to cook than white meat, so cook the legs separately from the body. If you want to leave them on, cut the skin between the breast and the legs and spread them out, away from the abdomen, to expose more of the leg to heat.

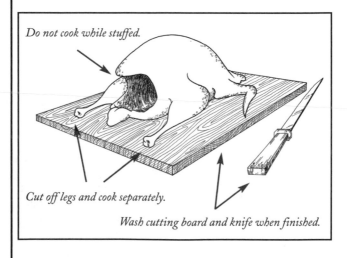

Do not cook while stuffed.

Cut off legs and cook separately.

Wash cutting board and knife when finished.

★ Cook the turkey breast-side down.
Cooking breast-side down will cause the juices to run down the sides and baste the breasts. Flip it over just before removing from the oven to crisp the skin.

How to Remove a Gravy Stain

Try the following techniques until one succeeds in removing the stain.

1 Remove excess food as soon as possible.
Use a spoon or a blunt knife to scrape the stain. The longer a stain sets, the more difficult it is to remove.

2 Make a detergent solution.
Mix one teaspoon of clear, mild liquid dishwashing detergent with one cup of lukewarm water. Do not use detergent that contains bleach.

3 Apply the detergent solution to the stain.
Do not rub the stain. Work from the edge of the stain in, gently blotting.

4 Rinse the stain with cold water and blot dry.
If the stain comes out, go to step 14.

5 Make an ammonia solution.
If the detergent solution does not work, mix one tablespoon of household ammonia with $1/2$ cup of warm water.

6   Apply the ammonia solution to the stain.
Blot the stain. Do not rub.

7   Rinse with cold water and blot dry.
If the stain now comes out, go to step 14.

8   Make a vinegar solution.
Mix $\frac{1}{3}$ cup white vinegar with $\frac{2}{3}$ cup cold water.

9   Blot the stain with the vinegar solution.

10   Rinse with cold water and blot dry.
If the stain has disappeared, go to step 14.

11   Apply commercial enzyme detergent.
Enzyme detergent is available in grocery, drug, and hardware stores. Blot the stain.

12   Rinse the area with cold water.

13   Blot dry.
Place a $\frac{1}{2}$-inch-thick pad of white paper towels over the stained area and weigh it down with a flat, heavy object—a thick book works well. Change the absorbent pad until the transfer of the stain is no longer visible on the pad.

14   Launder according to manufacturer's label.

HOW TO PUT OUT A GREASE FIRE

1 Do not douse with water.
Oil and water do not mix. Water will cause the burning oil to spatter and spread the fire. Do not move the burning pan to the sink.

2 Turn off the stove.

3 Put on an oven mitt.
Large mitts are the safest option. If barbecue mitts—those that cover the forearm—are available, use for added protection.

4 Find a lid that fits the pan.
A lid that is slightly larger than the pan will also work.

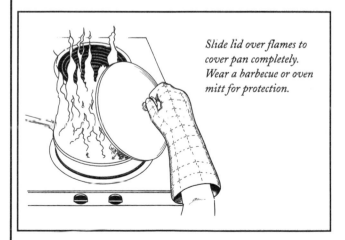

Slide lid over flames to cover pan completely. Wear a barbecue or oven mitt for protection.

5 Hold the lid at an angle toward the fire.
Do not try to lower the lid directly onto the pan or
you risk burning your arms. Keep your face and chest
as far from the flames as possible.

6 Slide the lid onto the pan and hold it in place until
the pan cools.
The pressure from the heat and flame can force a lid
off the pan. Hold it securely in place.

7 Do not lift the lid.
Lifting the lid will add oxygen and feed the fire. Take
the lid off only when the pan has become noticeably
cooler.

8 If no lid is available, use baking soda.
Dump a large amount of baking soda on the grease
fire to extinguish it quickly. Avoid using baking powder, which can cause the fire to flare.

Be Aware

- Do not use a dry chemical extinguisher to try to
  put out a grease fire. It is not effective, and the
  force of the compressed chemical agent can splat-
  ter burning material and spread flames.
- Never leave cooking oil to heat unattended:
  Flames may develop quickly.

How to Treat a Grease Burn

1 Cool the burned area.
Immediately run cold water over the burned area for several minutes or until the injury site is cool.

2 Dry the burned area gently.
Blot the injury site using a clean, dry towel or sheet.

3 Check for blistering.
If the blisters are small, pop them with a sterilized pin and remove dead skin using scissors. (Wiping the tip of a pin in alcohol or heating it in the flame from a match will adequately sterilize the pin.) If there are no blisters and the burn is less than one inch across, apply burn cream and a sterile dressing.

4 Cover severe burns.
If the burn is larger than one inch across or is very blistered, cover it with a clean, dry sheet or towel and seek medical attention promptly.

Be Aware

- Infection is the main risk. Signs of infection include fever or local warmth, increased redness around the burned area, increased soreness, red streaks, swelling, or drainage of pus.
- Do not apply oily or greasy substances such as petroleum jelly or butter to the wound. These popular but misguided burn remedies are detrimental to the healing process.

how to put out a grease fire

HOW TO REPURPOSE
A FRUITCAKE

★ Turn the fruitcake into another dessert.
Do not serve the fruitcake as is. Slice it very thin, tear the pieces apart, and use them in an English trifle, a dessert made with alternating layers of cake (née fruitcake), custard, whipped cream, and, sometimes, fresh fruit. Serve in a deep glass bowl (often called a trifle bowl).

★ Use the fruitcake as a doorstop.
Fruitcakes are very hardy and will last for years. Use the fruitcake to prop open a door.

★ Use the fruitcake to prevent your car from rolling.
When parked on a hill, wedge the fruitcake under the downhill side of a rear tire. In your garage, position the fruitcake on the floor as a tire stop to prevent the car from hitting the garage wall.

★ Use the fruitcake as a dumbbell.
A good-size fruitcake may weigh several pounds. Incorporate it into your exercise routine, holding it firmly for arm curls, or squeezing it between the feet for leg lifts.

★ Use the fruitcake in a carnival game.
Collect fruitcakes and stack them vertically in a pyramid. Using tennis balls, try to knock down the fruitcakes in five throws.

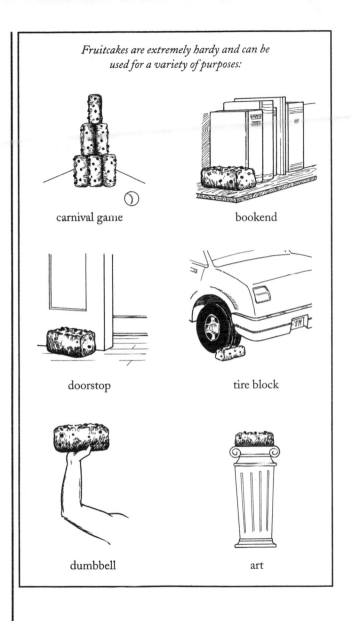

Fruitcakes are extremely hardy and can be used for a variety of purposes:

carnival game

bookend

doorstop

tire block

dumbbell

art

★ **Use as bookends.**
Set up two fruitcakes either horizontally or vertically, depending on the size of the books.

★ **Use as art.**
Bolt a fruitcake to a painted board, frame it and hang it on your wall, or simply place it on a pedestal. Position the fruitcake in a well-lit area.

★ **Use the fruitcake as compost.**
Fruitcakes are made of (mostly) organic material, and make good fertilizer. However, it may take several years for the fruitcake to decompose.

How to Safely Eat a Fruitcake

1 **Slice it thin.**
Cut the fruitcake into narrow slices—no more than $3/8$ inch—while the cake is cool. Place the slices on a serving platter, cover, and allow to come to room temperature.

2 **Check the knife.**
After cutting, the blade should be somewhat sticky and slightly colored. If the knife does not have to be wiped with a damp cloth after each cut, the cake is too dry, and a healthy dollop of whipped cream will be necessary. If the knife is heavily streaked with cake ingredients after cutting, the fruitcake has not been baked long enough and may need to be repurposed.

3 | **Disguise the taste.**
Cover with lots of ice cream and whipped cream. Wash the fruitcake down with strong black coffee, Irish coffee, brandy, or a hot toddy.

4 | **Swallow without chewing.**
Cut the slice into small pieces. Swallow each piece whole, as you would a vitamin. If chewing is necessary, use your molars, not your front teeth or incisors, and try not to touch the food with your tongue, which has all your taste buds.

Be Aware

- Do not be fooled by a gift of a "Yule cake," "Christmas ring," or "dried fruit bread"—these are just other names for a fruitcake.

- If the fruitcake is very dark in color, it contains lots of molasses and corn syrup, making it exceedingly sticky, thick, and dense. The heavier the fruitcake, the more candied fruit and dark molasses it has. The darker or heavier the fruitcake, the more difficult it will be to swallow.

- A light-colored fruitcake is a good sign; the cake has plenty of batter and light corn syrup.

- Fruitcake should be stored in a cool place, such as a refrigerator or cellar. If kept cool and in a tin, the cake will last for at least a year, and you can give it as a present the following Christmas.

HOW TO OPEN A BOTTLE OF WINE WITH A BROKEN CORK

1   **Examine the cork.**
If the cork has broken due to improper corkscrew use, treat the broken cork as if it were whole. If the cork is pushed too far into the bottle, push it all the way in using any long thin implement and proceed to "With a Very Dry Cork," step 5, below.

2   **Reinsert the corkscrew.**
Six half turns of the corkscrew will usually be enough to allow you to remove a full cork, but you may need fewer for a partial cork. Turn the corkscrew slowly to prevent further cork breakage.

3   **Pull the cork out.**
Pull up steadily on the corkscrew, being careful not to jerk the cork out of the bottle. If the cork remains in the bottle, go to "With a Very Dry Cork," step 2, below.

WITH A VERY DRY CORK

1   **Check for crumbling.**
If the cork is soft and powdery, it will not offer the corkscrew enough resistance. It may also be stuck to the sides of the bottle, making intact removal impossible.

  chapter 1: cooking and entertaining

2 | Bore a hole through the center of the cork.
Use the corkscrew as a drill.

3 | Widen the hole.
Wiggle the corkscrew from side to side to increase the diameter of the hole.

4 | Try to pour.
If the wine will not pour, continue to enlarge the diameter of the hole as above, or force the remainder of the cork into the bottle (see "How to Open a Bottle of Wine Without a Corkscrew," page 32).

5 | Make a filter.
Place a piece of clean, unwaxed, unbleached cheesecloth over the mouth of a decanter and secure it tightly with a rubber band. If no cheesecloth is available, use a coffee filter (preferably unbleached). Do not use a T-shirt or any article of clothing you have washed in detergent—the detergent can affect the taste of the wine.

6 | Strain the wine.
Carefully pour the wine through the filter into the decanter. When the bottle is empty, remove the filter containing the pieces of cork from the mouth of the decanter and serve the wine.

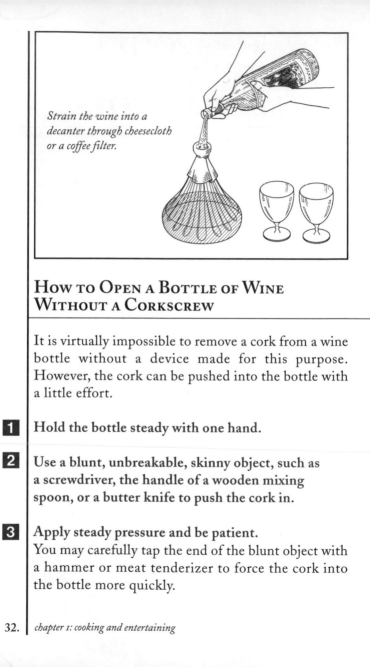

Strain the wine into a decanter through cheesecloth or a coffee filter.

How to Open a Bottle of Wine Without a Corkscrew

It is virtually impossible to remove a cork from a wine bottle without a device made for this purpose. However, the cork can be pushed into the bottle with a little effort.

1 Hold the bottle steady with one hand.

2 Use a blunt, unbreakable, skinny object, such as a screwdriver, the handle of a wooden mixing spoon, or a butter knife to push the cork in.

3 Apply steady pressure and be patient.
You may carefully tap the end of the blunt object with a hammer or meat tenderizer to force the cork into the bottle more quickly.

HOW TO AVOID SHOOTING A CHAMPAGNE CORK

1 Hold the thumb of your non-dominant hand over the cage and cork.

The cork may fly out of the bottle as soon as the wire mesh (known as the "cage") is loosened. Keep pressure on the cork and point the bottle away from yourself and anyone nearby.

2 Turn the key of the wire cage.

All cages on champagne and sparkling wine open after six clockwise half-turns. Remove the cage.

3 Place an opened cloth napkin over the cork and neck of the bottle.

Hold the bottle in your non-dominant hand and the napkin over the cork in your other hand. Keep the bottle angled away from people.

4 Hold the cork tightly and slowly turn the bottle clockwise.

Do not turn the cork or you risk breaking it.

5 As the cork begins to come out, apply downward pressure on it.

The pressure will prevent the cork from shooting away from the bottle.

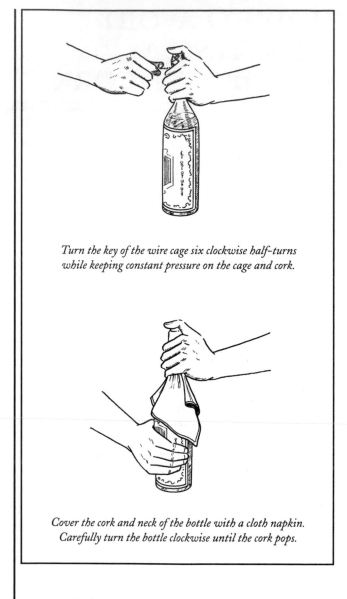

Turn the key of the wire cage six clockwise half-turns while keeping constant pressure on the cage and cork.

Cover the cork and neck of the bottle with a cloth napkin. Carefully turn the bottle clockwise until the cork pops.

chapter 1: cooking and entertaining

6 | Hold the cork at the mouth of the bottle for five seconds.
If champagne begins to bubble up and out, it will react with the end of the cork and flow back into the bottle.

7 | Slowly pour the champagne.
Pour the champagne slowly until the froth (called "mousse") reaches about $^2/_3$ up the glass, then pause. When the mousse has receded, continue filling until the glass is approximately $^2/_3$ full.

Be Aware

- The quieter the pop, the better the opening.
  A poor opening will cause champagne to spurt out of the bottle, resulting in lost champagne and carbonation.
- An uncontrolled opening may result in the cork leaving the champagne bottle with enough force to cause injury to someone nearby.
- Crystal flutes will improve the champagne experience: The slender shape makes the long streams of bubbles more visually appealing and concentrates the aroma. The finest leaded crystal (with a lead content of about 25 percent) has the smoothest surface and allows the champagne to maintain maximum carbonation.
- Never chill champagne flutes.
- Avoid champagne "saucers": Their larger surface area releases more carbonation.
- The smaller the bubbles, the better the champagne.

Never uncork a champagne bottle while facing a crowd.

CHAPTER 2
FRIENDS AND FAMILY

HOW TO DEAL WITH A MEDDLING PARENT

1 Prepare yourself mentally.
Remember that the holidays are a time for celebration, and try to maintain a positive attitude no matter what your parents may say.

2 If your parents give unwanted or annoying advice, be polite and attempt to change the subject.
Thank them for their concern. Say, "I appreciate your advice, but I'd really rather talk about [insert new subject here]."

3 Avoid confrontation.
Never respond to a meddling parent with phrases that include "you always," "you never," or "leave it alone." Suggest discussing the issue at another time. If you are a guest in someone else's home, confrontation should be avoided at all costs.

4 Smother the conversation with kindness.
Always counter a negative remark with a positive one. If your parent says, "Your house really needs painting," counter with, "This house is in such a great neighborhood. Isn't that great for the kids!" If your parent says, "When are you going to get a real job?" counter with, "I'm making great progress on my novel!"

5 Do not discuss money in public.

How much things cost and financial success are attractive topics for a meddling parent. These are inappropriate subjects for group conversation, however. Do not get angry; deflect the inquiry. If a question about money is asked, say, "I can't remember what we paid," or "We're just thankful for what we have."

6 Avoid taking the bait.

If a meddling parent keeps mentioning how well other people are doing compared to you—how important a job, how many children, how big a house—or makes other implicitly critical comparisons, just say, "That's wonderful."

7 Ask for their advice about a less-irritating topic.

Meddling parents often simply want to be asked for their opinions. Seeking their thoughts on a less important subject or even on a made-up problem may placate them or distract them from sensitive issues (ask for their input on remodeling the kitchen, for example, even if you are not intending to do so).

8 If the meddling parent will not relent, excuse yourself from the conversation.

Casually excuse yourself (do not say, "I can't listen to this anymore!") and move to another room. For example, finish your drink and say, "I need to get a refill" (do not offer to get your parent one); or say, "Excuse me, I have to go to the bathroom," or "I have to make a phone call," or "I promised I would help in the kitchen." Do not make any promises to come right back.

Be Aware

- It is best to preempt meddling parents by announcing lots of news before the holidays arrive. Phone or e-mail the week before with updates, keeping the news positive and upbeat.
- Remember that you do not have to answer every question. In advance of the holidays, practice non-responses or evasive responses, such as "Do you really think so?" or "That's an interesting question. Let me think about it." In front of a mirror, practice the blank stare.

HOW TO SURVIVE IF YOU HAVE NO ONE TO KISS ON NEW YEAR'S EVE

IF YOU ARE WITH OTHERS

1 Keep a glass in your hand.
If others think you are being festive and uninhibited, you are much more likely to receive a kiss. Even if you are not drinking, always hold a partly full glass of champagne.

2 Hug people.
As the clock strikes midnight, begin hugging everyone around you.

3 Select a desirable person.
As you are hugging, look for an attractive person who you would enjoy kissing and who might kiss you. If a person is not randomly kissing others, he or she may be less likely to kiss you.

4 Begin your approach.
Act casual, but keep your destination in view. Slowly move toward your chosen one, hugging everyone on the way.

5 Time your arrival.

Do not appear to be "lining up" to kiss this person. Time your arrival precisely as the person releases the previous reveler.

6 Yell first, then hug.

Yell "Happy New Year!" as you move in. Hug, embrace, then pull away slightly.

7 Kiss.

Keep your mouth closed, pucker slightly, and plant the kiss.

IF YOU ARE ALONE

 Kiss a pet.

Dogs are generally agreeable and have relatively clean mouths. Cats are usually well groomed but are more passive and tend to get rather than give. Keep your mouth closed.

 Kiss yourself.

Find a mirror, pucker up, lean close, and kiss. Keep the lips slightly parted. Do not attempt to use your tongue. Wipe the mirror clean after you have completed your kiss. You may also try kissing the back of your hand.

Kiss a celebrity.

Watch a favorite movie or show on television and kiss the screen when an appealing star has a close-up.

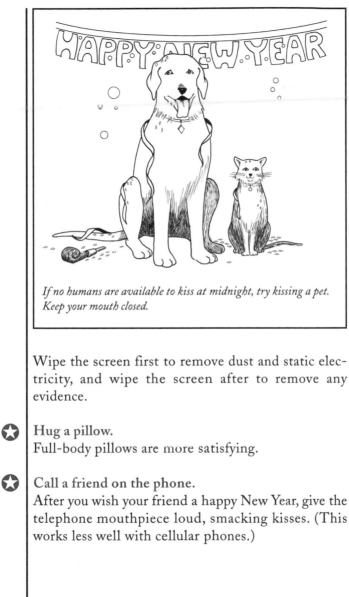

If no humans are available to kiss at midnight, try kissing a pet.
Keep your mouth closed.

Wipe the screen first to remove dust and static electricity, and wipe the screen after to remove any evidence.

⭐ Hug a pillow.
Full-body pillows are more satisfying.

⭐ Call a friend on the phone.
After you wish your friend a happy New Year, give the telephone mouthpiece loud, smacking kisses. (This works less well with cellular phones.)

HOW TO FEND OFF AN UNWANTED KISS

On Arrival

1 Carry a present, coat, hat, or child in front of you as you enter.

2 Extend your free arm in a wide arc and move into a hug position.

3 If the greeter leans in to plant a kiss, use the head-and-shoulders maneuver.
Move your head toward the kisser, then at the last moment, rotate your shoulders, throw your arm around, and bury your head in the kisser's neck.

Under the Mistletoe

1 Find the mistletoe.
As soon as you arrive, determine the location of the mistletoe. Check the lintel over doorways and hanging lights, which often obscure the mistletoe.

2 Establish alternate routes.
Avoiding the mistletoe is the best defense. Plan your comings and goings so that you do not pass under the mistletoe.

Carry a large present in your arms as you enter in order to block an unwanted kiss.

3 Employ evasive maneuvers.

If the mistletoe is hung in an inescapable location and someone is approaching, be prepared to use counter-measures:

- Keep walking, as if you didn't realize you were under the mistletoe.
- Carry a drink or plate of food at all times, and quickly take a sip or bite as the person approaches.

- Sneeze, cough, or scratch your nose just as the person moves in. When they hesitate, turn the attempted kiss into a friendly hug.
- Move rapidly and place a preemptive, glancing kiss on the person's forehead or cheek, thereby avoiding a more serious kiss.

4 Make up a mistletoe-related fib.

When fleeing from the would-be kisser seems too rude and other defensive tactics won't work, create a new mistletoe custom that would preclude the kiss:

- "This mistletoe has no berries! That's bad luck!"
- "That's not real mistletoe, it's plastic! How tacky—we can't kiss under that!"
- "Can you believe they put up mistletoe? Who believes in that anymore?"

Be Aware

- Portable mistletoe—a sprig attached to the end of a curved stick—is not valid mistletoe and does not invoke the kiss tradition. (You might also question why you are attending a party with someone who would attempt the "mistletoe-on-a-stick" trick.)
- Do not attempt to avoid a mistletoe kiss by claiming that you are not Christian. The custom of kissing under mistletoe is not specific to Christianity and is observed in many religions and countries.

HOW TO OVERCOME HOLIDAY DEPRESSION

1 Avoid excess.
Overdoing certain things can promote depression. To prevent the onset of depression:
- Avoid increased stress.
- Avoid increased consumption of alcohol and sugar.
- Avoid poor eating habits and nutritional deficiencies.
- Avoid increased spending and financial burdens.
- Avoid overwhelming social commitments.

2 Eat mood-elevating foods.
L-tryptophane and L-tyrosine, two amino acids, are essential for the production of the mood elevator seratonin. Two natural sources of L-tryptophane are pumpkin seeds and turkey, while L-tryosine can be found in dairy products, beans, meat, and fish. To support the nervous system and help resolve stress, take B-complex vitamins. Since low levels of magnesium can cause depression, eat green vegetables, since magnesium is part of the chlorophyll complex.

3 Exercise.
Take brisk walks or exercise vigorously. Strenuous exercise increases endorphin levels and elevates the mood. Activity also helps flush the lymphatic system and remove wastes that can adversely affect mood. Exercising outdoors in sunlight is also a mood enhancer.

4 Focus on the brevity of the holiday.
Even the longest day has only 24 hours.

5 Embrace the pain.
Instead of trying to avoid holiday activities (cooking, shopping, cleaning, traveling) or wallowing passively in your depression, actively embrace the very things you dread. This counter-intuitive approach will surprise others as well as yourself, and may shock your system into a better mood. It will also pass the time more quickly.

HOW TO DEAL WITH POST-HOLIDAY DEPRESSION

1 Remove all holiday decorations.
Holiday decorations, while attractive, can also serve to remind you of the celebration that is now a part of the past. Take them down and pack them away.

2 Return all unwanted gifts as soon as possible.
Unwanted gifts that remain in the house only serve as painful reminders of the holidays. Replace these items with new things that you genuinely want, and be happy with your new acquisitions.

3 Recognize the symptoms of post-holiday depression.
The symptoms include apathy toward work, social events, relationships, and goals; loss of energy, appetite, self-esteem; feelings of guilt, hopelessness, or free-floating anxiety; excessive or interrupted sleep; and frequent headaches. Accepting the fact that you

have post-holiday depression is the first step toward dealing with it.

4 Plan another event.
Look ahead to birthdays, trips, anniversaries, and other occasions you can celebrate soon.

5 Think about next year.
Remind yourself that your favorite holidays will be back again next year. Focus on how much fun you will have then.

6 Eat mood-elevating foods and exercise.
See "How to Overcome Holiday Depression," steps 2 and 3, page 47.

Be Aware

- Holiday depression, stress, and anxiety often arise from letting things go until the last minute or from overspending. Plan and spend accordingly.
- Herbal mood elevators include St. John's wort, skullcap and oats, kava kava and valerian root, milk thistle, and the Chinese herb Hsiao Yao Wan. Use as directed.
- An underactive thyroid gland can cause depression. If none of the above remedies are successful, have your thyroid checked.
- Many people suffer from seasonal affective disorder (SAD), which results from exposure to fewer hours of sunlight. It might be the season, not the holidays, that are at the root of your dissatisfaction.

HOLIDAY EMERGENCIES

HOW TO TREAT FOOD POISONING

1   Stay hydrated.
The symptoms of food poisoning vary depending on the type of microorganism or toxin ingested, but can generally cause severe stomach cramping, fever, vomiting, and diarrhea, leading to dehydration. Drink several gallons of water per day.

2   Replenish mineral salts.
Eat bland foods, in moderation, as soon as you are able. Diarrhea depletes the body of salts, and drinking water alone will not replace them; sports rehydration drinks are effective. Nibble on dry salted crackers or plain rice to replenish salts, too.

3   Do not induce vomiting.
Depending on the microorganism or toxin involved, food poisoning may cause vomiting, which does not clear the bacteria from the body, but will cause further dehydration.

4   Do not take anti-peristaltic medication.
Some anti-diarrhea medications work by slowing the movement of waste in the gut, causing the toxins to remain in the body for a longer period of time.

5 Avoid alcohol, spicy foods, and milk products.
These drinks and foods may aggravate the gut and cause additional gas and cramping. Never follow a suspect meal with a drink of alcohol to "kill" the germs; this is not effective.

6 Be prepared for several days of discomfort.
Food poisoning may induce a severe headache and sweating. Keep the body cool: Never try to sweat out the germs. The symptoms of food poisoning are usually short-lived. If the symptoms persist for more than a week, or if you detect bleeding, consult a health care professional.

HOLIDAY FOOD ALERT

⭐ Oysters should be fully cooked.
Raw oysters are particularly susceptible to invasions by microorganisms that can cause food poisoning: If the raw oyster tastes "off" in any way, do not swallow it.

⭐ Fully cook all meat.
Poultry should be fully cooked, with no traces of pink or red, to an internal temperature of 165° F. Beef and game should be cooked to at least 140° F.

⭐ Serve cooked foods immediately.
Cooked foods that are not served immediately must be kept at a holding temperature between 140° and 165° F. Do not leave food unrefrigerated longer than two hours or the chances of bacterial growth increase.

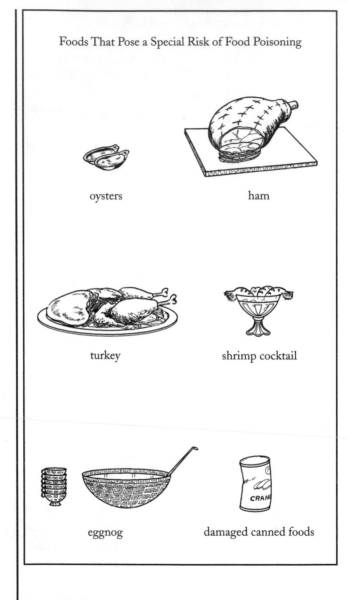

Foods That Pose a Special Risk of Food Poisoning

oysters

ham

turkey

shrimp cocktail

eggnog

damaged canned foods

★ Egg yolks should not be eaten raw or runny.
This will reduce the risk of salmonella poisoning.
Eggnog usually contains raw egg yolks, so make sure
the eggnog you drink has been pasteurized. Homemade
mayonnaise is made with raw eggs, so avoid it.

★ Cooked shellfish should be kept on ice.
Fish and seafood, especially shellfish, are often har-
bor to many different kinds of microorganisms.

★ Avoid any dented cans.
If the seal on the can has been affected, the contents
may be contaminated and you risk getting botulism.

Be Aware

- Food poisoning is caused by a range of microorganisms or their byproducts. Each bug has its
  own properties and set of symptoms: Some must
  be alive and present in large quantities to cause
  harm, while others, such as *E. coli* 0157, can inflict
  a lethal dose from just a few bacteria.
- Separate raw and cooked foods. Even foods that
  have been properly cooked can be contaminated
  if they come in contact with raw foods or implements (knives and cutting boards, for example)
  that have touched them.
- Drink bottled water when traveling to visit rela-
  tives if you are unsure of the safety of the tap
  water. Avoid ice cubes, as these are usually made
  with tap water. Check seals on bottles to make
  sure they are intact: If they are broken, the bottles
  may have been refilled with tap water.

HOW TO EXTINGUISH A CHRISTMAS TREE FIRE

1 Assess the size and nature of the fire.

Quickly determine if the source of the fire is electrical, and observe how large an area of the tree is burning. A fire larger than the size of a small wastebasket cannot usually be contained, even with a home extinguisher. If the fire is that large, evacuate the building and call the fire department from a cellular phone or a neighbor's house.

2 If the fire is small and not electrical, douse it or smother it.

Extinguish the fire with a bucket of water or a multipurpose (Class ABC) fire extinguisher, or smother it with a wet blanket.

3 If the fire is electrical, use a fire extinguisher.

Do not throw water on an electrical fire. Use a multipurpose (Class ABC) home fire extinguisher.

4 When using a fire extinguisher, stand with your back toward an exit, six to eight feet from the fire, and Pull, Aim, Squeeze, Sweep (PASS).

Pull the release tab, aim at the base of the fire, squeeze the lever to release the pressurized chemicals, and sweep from side to side as you slowly move closer to the fire.

If the fire is larger than the size of a small wastebasket or is spreading quickly, get out of the house.

5 | If the fire is still spreading, exit the house.
Evacuate the building quickly. Do not attempt to save ornaments, Christmas presents, or other valuables.

How to Prevent a Christmas Tree Fire

1 | Select a fresh tree.
A dry tree is a major fire hazard; to get the freshest tree, cut it yourself. If you purchase a precut tree, run your hand down a branch to make sure it is not dry and shedding needles. Test the tree by bending a needle: If it snaps, the tree is too dry.

2 | Leave the tree in a bucket of water overnight.
Place the tree in the stand the next day. Water it daily.

3 | Place the tree at least three feet away from a fireplace, radiator, or other heat source.

4 | Unplug tree lights when not in use.
Do not leave the lights on during the day, when you go to bed, or when you leave the house.

5 | Do not place lit candles on or near a tree.
If tradition requires candles, use specially weighted sconces that do not tip over. Do not add electric tree lights or other electric equipment to or around the tree (such as a train set), in the event that water must be thrown onto the tree. Do not leave the tree unattended.

HOW TO SURVIVE A FALL FROM A LADDER

1 Anticipate the fall.
As soon as you feel the ladder or stepstool move or you begin to lose your balance, be ready to shift your position. You will have less than a second to react.

2 Do not grab at any fixtures or decorations.
Lighting fixtures, decorations, hooks, and wires will not support your body weight—just prepare for impact.

3 Position your body.
As you begin to fall, twist your body so your back is to the ground.

Do not grab any fixtures or decorations on the way down. Curl into a ball and land on your backside.

4 Curl into a ball.

Tucking in your arms and legs and curling into a ball will minimize the chance of breaking any limbs. The longer the fall, the more time you will have to prepare.

5 Attempt to land on your rear.

The safest part of the body to land on is the backside. This landing will minimize major damage, including broken heels and spinal cord injuries.

Be Aware

- A backside landing can cause a tailbone fracture or a vertebral compression fracture, but neither of these usually results in life-long disability.
- If you are on a taller ladder, do not try to land on your feet. While leg and ankle fractures are generally short-term injuries, heel (calcaneus) fractures have an extended recovery time and can cause long-term disability.
- If you are stranded on a roof with no way to get down and no one in sight, shout down the chimney. If there is a fire in the fireplace, however, do not inhale smoke between shouts.

HOW TO SURVIVE CHRISTMAS TREE LIGHT DISASTERS

How to Untangle Christmas Tree Lights

1 Remain calm.
Untangling tree lights can be a frustrating and prolonged process. Wear loose-fitting, comfortable clothing; turn on cheerful music; and sit in a comfortable chair. Trying to work quickly will only make you more frustrated and result in further tangles.

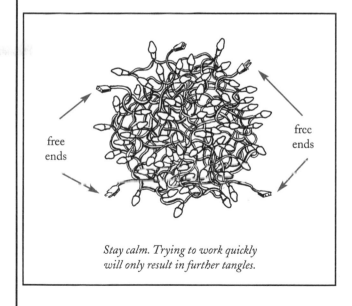

free
ends

free
ends

Stay calm. Trying to work quickly will only result in further tangles.

2 Unplug all connected strands.
Light strands plugged into one another can create a very complex, knotted loop. Unplug all strands so that your tangle contains several separate sections.

3 Find a free end.
Do not attempt to untangle the lights from the center of the knotted mass. If there is more than one free end, pick one.

4 Loosen all the knots.
Splay your fingers open within the tangles of the knots to loosen them. When the knots are all loose, open a hole through the tangle to separate the free end from the mass.

5 Wind the free end methodically back through each knot.
Do not yank on the free end; gently work it through the untangled knots. Always treat the strands gently to avoid breaking the bulbs.

6 Untie each successive knot carefully.
Keep the free end rolled to make it easier to work with and to reduce the length of cord you need to pass through the knots.

7 Keep the free end under control.
Never pull on the free end. Pulling will tighten the tangle and make the knots harder to untie. As you work, the knot-free section should continue to get longer. Even if the tangle seems to be getting more severe, if the knot-free section is lengthening, you will ultimately succeed.

8 Repeat as necessary.
Once one strand of lights has been removed from the
tangle, repeat the process with another free end until
each strand is removed and the tangle eliminated.
Keep yourself hydrated.

Be Aware
• The best way to prevent light strands from tangling
  is to coil them around a stiff piece of cardboard
  before putting them away.
• Severcly knotted strands may take hours to untangle.
  If you do not wish to spend time in this manner,
  consider buying new lights. The cost of tree lights
  has dropped considerably in recent years.

How to Respond to Prolonged Tree-Light Shock

Faulty lights or extension cords may pose a risk of
electrocution.

1 Do not touch a victim still connected to the power
source.
Shut off power at the breaker/fuse box as quickly as
possible. You must eliminate the power source before
handling the light string or touching the victim. Once
the power is off, it is safe to touch the victim.

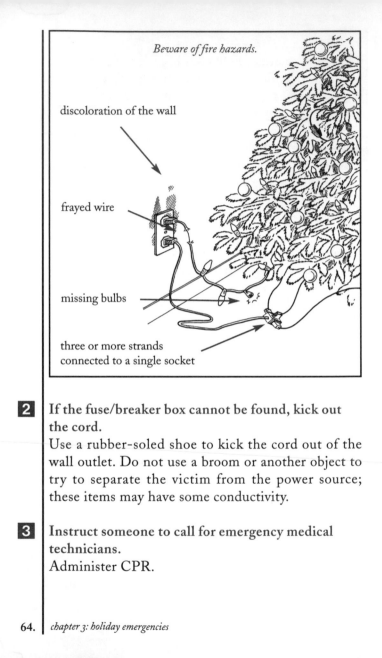

Beware of fire hazards.

discoloration of the wall

frayed wire

missing bulbs

three or more strands
connected to a single socket

2 If the fuse/breaker box cannot be found, kick out
the cord.
Use a rubber-soled shoe to kick the cord out of the
wall outlet. Do not use a broom or another object to
try to separate the victim from the power source;
these items may have some conductivity.

3 Instruct someone to call for emergency medical
technicians.
Administer CPR.

Be Aware

- Never connect more than three strands to a single socket. Count an extension cord as one strand.

- Check the condition of all light strands. Look for frayed wire, cuts, and cracking of the cords. Discard any lights in poor condition, or any strands with rusting sockets.

- Use light strands that have been approved by a certified testing lab.

- To reduce shock risk, always keep bulbs in all light sockets. Newer strands will light even with burned out or defective bulbs: Either replace the bad bulb before using the lights or leave the burnt bulb in place. Make sure connections between strands are tight.

- Check the outlet and wall area around it for discoloration, which may be a sign that the outlet is faulty.

- Light strands may be slightly warm to the touch; this is not unusual. However, if they are hot, unplug and replace them, or use another outlet.

- Never coil light strands when they are connected to power; this will generate heat and may cause a fire. Unplug lights during the day to reduce heat buildup.

- If using outdoor lights, wrap connections between strands with electrical tape, and make sure connetions at the power source are protected from moisture.

- Plugging light strands into a surge protector does not offer protection from electric shock. These devices are designed to protect property from current spikes or surges, not to protect people from the current leakages that cause electric shock.

HOW TO RESIZE A CHRISTMAS TREE

If It Is Too Tall for the Room

1 Do not force it inside.
Keep the tree outdoors or in another room until you have made the necessary alterations.

2 Obtain pruning shears and a bow saw.
Prepare to use long-handled, scissor-type shears for removing branches, and an open-throated bow saw with a 20- or 30-inch steel blade for cutting a large trunk.

3 Measure the height of the tree stand, the tree itself, and the height of the room.
Figure out approximately how much shorter the tree needs to be.

4 Locate the whorl and internodal branches.
Whorl branches are larger in diameter and grow out from the trunk in sets of four to six; they resemble the spokes of wheel. Sets of whorl branches are located every 12 to 15 inches along the trunk of a standard eight-foot-tall tree. Internodal branches are smaller in diameter and are randomly spaced on the tree between the whorl branches.

Pull tree inside house trunk first. Do not force tree through doorway.

5 | Mark the tree for cutting.
Find the lowest level of whorl branches whose removal will sufficiently shorten the tree but will leave enough space for the trunk to neatly fit into the tree stand. Make a hash mark with the saw just above these whorl branches on the trunk.

6 | Remove the branches below your hash mark to prepare the trunk for trimming.
Use the shears for branches up to 1 inch in diameter, and use the bow saw for larger branches. Without branches, the trunk will be easier to cut.

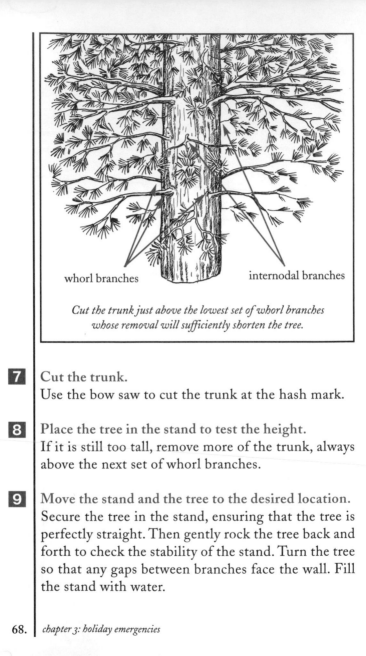

whorl branches   internodal branches

Cut the trunk just above the lowest set of whorl branches
whose removal will sufficiently shorten the tree.

7 Cut the trunk.
Use the bow saw to cut the trunk at the hash mark.

8 Place the tree in the stand to test the height.
If it is still too tall, remove more of the trunk, always
above the next set of whorl branches.

9 Move the stand and the tree to the desired location.
Secure the tree in the stand, ensuring that the tree is
perfectly straight. Then gently rock the tree back and
forth to check the stability of the stand. Turn the tree
so that any gaps between branches face the wall. Fill
the stand with water.

If It Is Too Wide for the Stand

1 Measure the diameter of the stand and the diameter of the tree.

2 Incrementally taper the trunk until it fits the stand. Use a bow saw to remove strips of bark and trunk, cutting parallel to the trunk. Remove equal amounts from all sides of the tree.

Be Aware
Do not attempt to use an electric carving knife to taper the trunk.

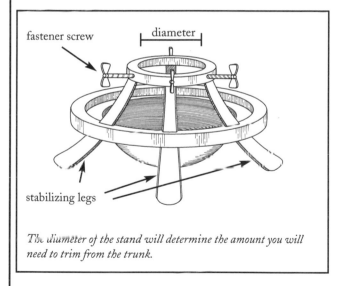

The diameter of the stand will determine the amount you will need to trim from the trunk.

HOW TO PREVENT A TREE FROM TOPPLING OVER

How to Make an Untippable Tree Stand

1 Obtain 6-inch diameter PVC pipe and cut it to 15 inches long.

2 Stand the pipe in the center of an empty 5-gallon plastic bucket.

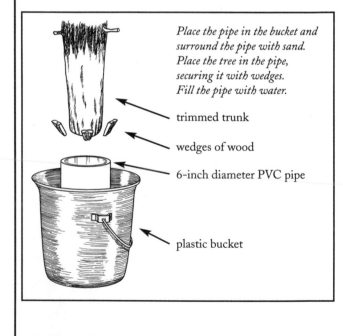

Place the pipe in the bucket and surround the pipe with sand. Place the tree in the pipe, securing it with wedges. Fill the pipe with water.

trimmed trunk

wedges of wood

6-inch diameter PVC pipe

plastic bucket

3 Fill the bucket, around the pipe, with sand.

4 Place the tree in the pipe.
The trunk should be free of branches on the bottom 15 inches. (See "If It Is Too Wide for the Stand," page 69, for trimming instructions.)

5 Secure the tree in the pipe with small wedges of wood. Cut the wedges out of branches you removed earlier. Set them around the trunk at the opening of the pipe to hold it in place.

6 Fill the pipe with water.
Water may leak from the bottom of the pipe into the sand. Monitor the water level to ensure the tree stays moist. This stand will hold a 9-foot tree. Use a larger bucket and a longer pipe for a bigger tree.

How to Make a Ceiling Guy Wire

1 Tie metal picture wire or heavyweight fishing line to the top of the tree.
Tie a short length of wire to the main trunk, just below the top of the tree.

2 Screw a hook into the ceiling directly above the tree.

3 Thread the wire through the ceiling hook and pull taut.

4 Knot the line securely.

Secure the tree with fishing line or wire.

HOW TO MAKE WALL GUY WIRES

Secure two wires to the trunk a third of the way down the tree.

Tie the free end of each wire to a hook attached to the wall on either side of the tree. Alternatively, loop a single wire around the trunk and attach each end to the wall hooks.

Be Aware

Cut tree branches have many uses. Place them under the tree to cover the stand, or use them to make wreathes or window box decorations.

HOW TO TREAT MISTLETOE POISONING

Discovery of partially chewed mistletoe, or the symptoms of mistletoe poisoning, calls for different responses for pets and humans.

1 Determine if real berries have been ingested.
Ingesting large numbers of real berries can cause a rapid increase in blood pressure that can lead to cardiac arrest. For this reason, many mistletoe distributors often replace the natural berries with plastic ones, which are light-colored and waxy looking. Check the mistletoe to see if the remaining berries are real; if they are, go to step 3.

2 Look for missing or chewed leaves.
Mistletoe leaves contain less of the toxins (tyramine and beta-phenethylamine) found in berries, but present another danger: Leaves have a protein toxin (phoratoxin) that causes severe gastrointestinal pain, cramping, and diarrhea. Unlike berries, leaves on packaged mistletoe are generally not plastic. The most common mistletoe leaves in the United States (*Phoradendron tomentosum*) are $1/2$ to 2 inches long, smooth-edged, leathery, and green. These oblong leaves sprout in pairs from opposite sides of the stem. European mistletoe (*Viscum album*) has larger and thinner leaves that are less green.

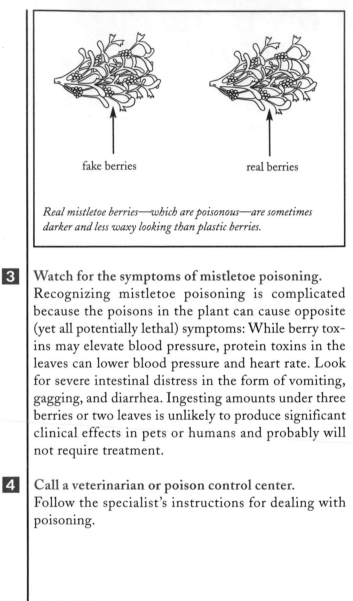

fake berries   real berries

Real mistletoe berries—which are poisonous—are sometimes darker and less waxy looking than plastic berries.

3 Watch for the symptoms of mistletoe poisoning.
Recognizing mistletoe poisoning is complicated because the poisons in the plant can cause opposite (yet all potentially lethal) symptoms: While berry toxins may elevate blood pressure, protein toxins in the leaves can lower blood pressure and heart rate. Look for severe intestinal distress in the form of vomiting, gagging, and diarrhea. Ingesting amounts under three berries or two leaves is unlikely to produce significant clinical effects in pets or humans and probably will not require treatment.

4 Call a veterinarian or poison control center.
Follow the specialist's instructions for dealing with poisoning.

Induce vomiting.
Vomiting should be induced unless two or more hours
have passed since mistletoe ingestion.
- Use 1 teaspoon of syrup of ipecac per 10 pounds
  of animal.
- If ipecac is unavailable, induce vomiting with 3-
  percent hydrogen peroxide. Administer 1 to 3
  teaspoons every 10 minutes a total of three times.
- If neither ipecac nor hydrogen peroxide is available, use ½ to 1 teaspoon of salt, placed directly
  on the back of the animal's tongue.

Coat the stomach.
If the pet ingested the mistletoe more than two hours
ago, attempt to slow the plant's absorption by the
body. Do not induce vomiting.
- Mix one tablet of activated charcoal per 2
  teaspoons of water. Administer 1 teaspoon of
  the solution per 2 pounds of animal, followed by
  several cups of water. Do not use ipecac.
- After half an hour, administer 1 teaspoon of
  milk of magnesia per five pounds of animal. If
  unavailable, administer vegetable oil, egg whites,
  or milk to coat the gastrointestinal tract.

If the symptoms do not subside within four hours,
take your pet to the veterinarian.

In People

1 Determine if the berries are real or not and ascertain what part of the plant has been consumed (see pages 73 and 74).

2 Call a poison control center immediately.
In the U.S., call 800-222-1222. Be prepared to tell the operator approximately how many leaves and (real) berries were ingested. The operator will instruct you on what to do. Do not administer pet rescue techniques to people.

Be Aware

- When administering help to your pet, be gentle—your pet is likely to be in distress. Be on guard for biting or wild behavior. Do not put your finger down your pet's throat to induce vomiting.

- When hanging mistletoe, consider placing it inside a piece of stocking (pantyhose) or a sealed sandwich bag to prevent any berries and leaves from falling to the floor, where they present a danger to pets and children.

- Poinsettias contain a latex sap that can irritate sensitive skin, and if ingested they may cause a burning sensation and intestinal disturbances, but they are not nearly as toxic as mistletoe.

HOW TO MAKE AN EMERGENCY MENORAH

If Hanukkah arrives and you are without a menorah
or candles, you will have to make your own. (See page
80 for making candles.)

BAKED MENORAH

You will need 2 cups flour, 1 cup salt, 1 cup water,
9 nuts or washers (at least $\frac{1}{2}$ inch in diameter), a large
mixing bowl, and at least three hours.

1 Preheat the oven to 200° F.

2 Mix the flour and salt together in the large bowl.

3 Add water.
Slowly pour water into the mixture and stir until it
becomes the consistency of dough. If it is too dry, add
more water; if it is too wet, add more flour.

4 Roll the dough into a strip about 12 inches long, 1
to 2 inches wide, and 2 inches thick.

5 Cut a 1-inch piece off one end and press it into the center of the strip.

The center area will be raised slightly: It will hold the Shamos candle, which is used to light the other candles.

6 Add the nuts to the dough.

Press the nuts into the dough, four spaced evenly on each side of the Shamos holder. Place the ninth nut in the raised center portion. The nuts should be pushed in so that part of the nut sticks up above the top of the dough. The nuts are the candle holders.

7 Bake.

Place the menorah on a baking sheet, and place in the oven. Bake for about two hours. The menorah is ready when the dough becomes hard. (You can air dry the menorah instead of baking it; allow two to three days for hardening.)

8 Let cool.

The menorah should be completely cool before use.

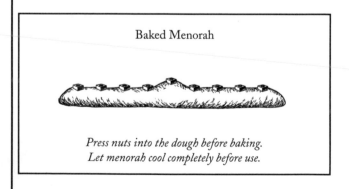

Baked Menorah

Press nuts into the dough before baking.
Let menorah cool completely before use.

Bowl and Dirt Menorah

You will need a baking dish or bowl and sand, dirt, rice, or gravel.

⭐ Fill a 2-inch-deep (or deeper) bowl with sand, dirt, rice, gravel, or other nonflammable material. Stick the appropriate number of candles in the dish each night (placing the Shamos on a slightly elevated mound) to create a makeshift menorah.

Be Aware

Do not make a menorah out of wood. Hanukkah candles must be allowed to burn down completely, and wood presents the risk of fire.

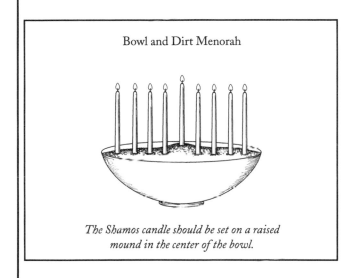

Bowl and Dirt Menorah

The Shamos candle should be set on a raised mound in the center of the bowl.

how to make an emergency menorah

HOW TO MAKE MENORAH CANDLES FROM CRAYONS

You will need 4 cups distilled water; 8 tablespoons boric acid; 4 tablespoons salt; 26 feet of string, twine, or cotton yarn; cardboard; an empty metal coffee can; a saucepan larger than the coffee can; heavy-duty foil; 44 steel washers; and 137 crayons.

1 Prepare a mordanting solution for the wick.
Mix the distilled water, boric acid (Borax), and salt in the large saucepan. This mordanting solution will minimize smoke and ash. Bring the solution to a boil.

2 Soak the string in the mordanting solution.
Submerge the string, twine, or cotton yarn in the boiling solution, remove from the heat, and let steep for four to eight hours.

3 Remove the string and hang to dry overnight.
Hang the string on the back of a folding chair, on a doorknob, or from a curtain rod. Ensure that loops of the string do not touch one another. Discard the mordanting solution and rinse the saucepan.

Crayons into Candles

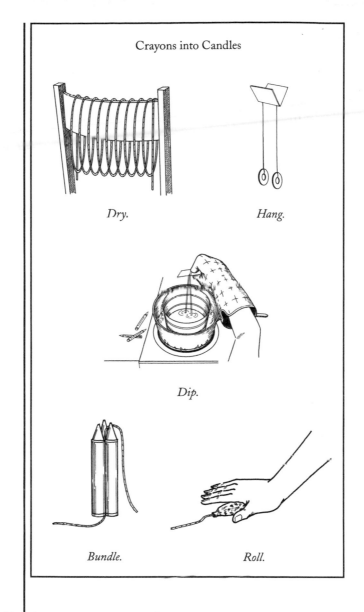

Dry.

Hang.

Dip.

Bundle.

Roll.

how to make menorah candles from crayons

4 When the string is completely dry, cut 22 strands, each 14 inches long.

Each strand will make a wick for two 6-inch candles at a time. Weight both ends of each length by tying on steel washers. These will keep the wick straight as the candle dries.

5 Prepare the wicks for dipping.

Drape each string piece over a 2-by-2-inch piece of cardboard folded in half, leaving equal lengths on either side. Cut slashes on opposite sides of the cardboard and lodge the wick into the slashes. Set aside.

6 Place the coffee can in the saucepan on the stovetop.

Fill the saucepan around the can with 3 to 4 inches of water. Bring the water to a boil, adding more water as necessary to keep the level constant.

7 Melt five crayons in the coffee can.

Remove all paper from the crayons before melting them. This wax will only be used to coat the wick, not to make the candles.

8 Dip two wicks.

Leave the wicks in the melted crayons until they are coated; 30 seconds is sufficient. Remove from the can and hang to dry.

9 Once dry, cut the string.

Remove the cardboard and washers and cut the string so that you have two prepared wicks, each about 7 inches long.

10 Stack three additional crayons around each wick. Remove the paper from the crayons first. This arrangement will form your candle. Allow a few extra inches of wick to protrude at each end.

11 Wrap the bundle tightly in several layers of heavy-duty aluminum foil.
A few layers will be necessary to prevent leaking.

12 Repeat steps 10 and 11 until all 44 candles are prepared.

13 Heat.
Place the foil-wrapped bundles on a baking sheet and put in a preheated 200° F oven for 20 minutes to fuse them together.

14 Shape.
When the bundles are warm and pliable to the touch, roll until the candles are the proper diameter to fit your menorah.

15 Remove the foil.

16 Set the candles.
Place them in the refrigerator for 30 minutes to cool.

Be Aware
Crayon-based candles are very smoky, drippy, and tend not to burn evenly. Watch them carefully when lit.

HOW TO MAKE AN EMERGENCY ANGEL

If you do not have an angel or ornaments for your Christmas tree, you will have to make your own.

PAPER PLATE ANGEL

You will need a paper plate, crayons or coloring pencils, a coffee mug, a quarter, scissors, and glue or tape.

1 Draw the angel.
In the center of the paper plate, trace the circumference of the mug for the wings and trace the quarter on the top inside edge of the first circle for the head, as shown. Draw in the shoulders freehand.

2 Cut on the bold lines as illustrated.
Keep the body attached to the skirt. The upper portion will fall away.

3 Decorate the angel with crayons or colored pencils.

4 Overlap the edges of the skirt behind the angel's back and tape or glue into place.
If you have no tape or glue, cut two vertical slits: one at the top of the left side, the other at the bottom of the right. Interlock the two sides.

5 Set the angel atop the tree.

chapter 3: holiday emergencies

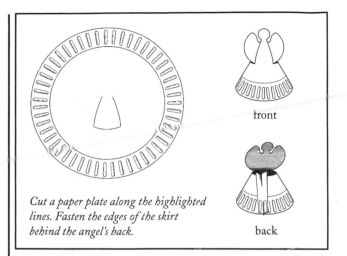

Cut a paper plate along the highlighted lines. Fasten the edges of the skirt behind the angel's back.

front

back

ALUMINUM FOIL ANGEL

You will need aluminum foil and a toilet paper tube.

1 Make the wings.
Cut a piece of foil approximately a foot and a half long. Fold it lengthwise like a fan, in alternating directions as illustrated. Hold the fan together in the center and spread out the foil in a wing-like manner.

2 Make the body.
Cut another piece of foil the same size and wrap it around the toilet paper tube, aligning one end of the foil with one edge of the tube; let the rest hang off. After rolling the tube in the foil, bunch the extra foil at one end to form the head. If the head seems too small, wrap another piece of tin foil around it to enlarge.

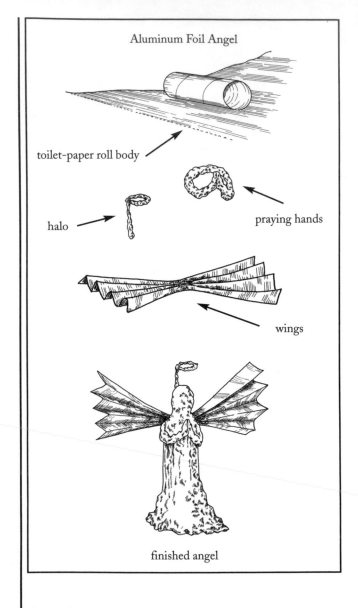

Aluminum Foil Angel

toilet-paper roll body

halo

praying hands

wings

finished angel

3 | Make a skirt.
Tear a strip of foil approximately five inches wide and wrap it around the tube to form a skirt. Bunch the skirt together in the back to hold it in place.

4 | Make a halo.
Tear a thin strip of foil. Make a ring at one end with the trailing piece coming straight down. Press the trailing piece into the crevices of the angel's head at the back.

5 | Make praying hands.
Tear another thin strip of foil approximately eight inches long. Wrap it around the angel's body, near the top of the tube. Press the ends together to form praying hands. Tear off any excess.

6 | Attach the wings.
Center the fan on the angel's upper back and press into the foil below the head to attach.

7 | Set the angel atop the tree.

ALTERNATIVE ORNAMENTS

Readily available items from home or a convenience store can be used as ornaments in an emergency.
- CDs—free-trial Internet providers' CDs or old music CDs create glittery reflective surfaces.
- Costume jewelry—earrings, brooches, and rings for ornaments, necklaces for tinsel.

how to make an emergency angel

- Clothing—scarves, lace undergarments, and anything for infants, especially hats, gloves, and shoes.
- Bread products—bagels or powdered-sugar donuts (around branches); white bread shaped into animals, balls, snowmen, or Santa; cookies; and fruitcakes (sliced).
- Lapel buttons—political or rock-and-roll pins, stuck or clipped to branches.

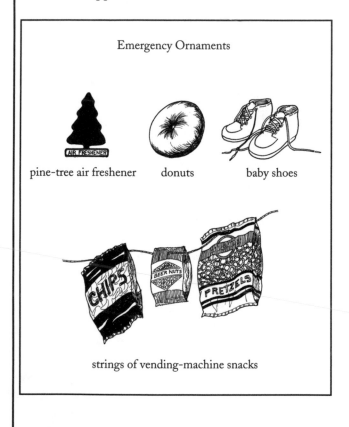

Emergency Ornaments

pine-tree air freshener   donuts   baby shoes

strings of vending-machine snacks

- Fruits and vegetables—jalapeño peppers, cherry tomatoes, zucchini, pearl onions, garlic cloves, and olives (with or without pimiento).
- Photographs—pictures of your family, photos of someone else's family or of celebrities torn out of magazines.
- Snack foods—vending machine-sized bags of chips, cookies, and candy, strung together.
- Air fresheners—automobile fresheners, shaped like pine trees, in a variety of colors.
- Gumdrops or gelatin-based candies—hung individually, strung together, or licked and stuck together in festive shapes.

Be Aware
- Perishables such as lunch meats, cheeses, and giblets pose potential health risks, and therefore do not make good decorative items.
- Use tape, grocery store twist-ties, paper clips, or thread if you do not have hangers.

HOW TO FIT INTO CLOTHING THAT IS TOO TIGHT

FOR MEN

1 Wear newer shirts and pants.
Garments (especially shirts) that have been laundered repeatedly are smaller than their original sizes. These items may also have loose buttons that might be ejected during a meal.

2 Choose dark-colored garments.
Lighter colors are less forgiving visually, while darker colors tend to obscure bulges.

3 Move your collar button.
Many men carry extra weight in the neck and jowls. Remove and reattach your collar button, moving it to the very edge of the collar tab. Wear a standard tie (not a bow tie) to hide the alteration.

4 Wear suits.
Suits are very effective for hiding pounds. They even out lines and offer structure to the body shape. Choose a dark-colored suit with a boxy shape rather than one cut narrow through the chest and waist. Shoulder padding is slimming, and is a must to balance the hips. (Broad shoulders help to create the

For Men

DO	DON'T
Move your collar button.	*Wear fitted shirts.*
Wear dark-colored, boxy suits.	*Wear horizontal stripes.*
Use the proper belt notch.	*Wear single-vented suits.*

ideal inverted triangle physique.) A suit jacket is also effective for hiding a large rear end: Choose a jacket with side vents/slits for extra room and comfort.

5 Move pants to below the belly.
Do not attempt to hike pants up and wear them high on the waist: This will result in an unsightly bulge, the pants may not close properly, and they will be too short in length. Wear them low on the hips, and use a jacket or loose-fitting shirt to conceal the gut.

6 Use the proper belt notch.
A belt should be worn in the third or fourth notch. Buy a longer belt rather than moving to a lower notch.

Be Aware
- Avoid fitted, knitted, polo-type tops, such as golf shirts. These garments accentuate what you want to hide.
- Avoid horizontal stripes, which widen your appearance.
- Avoid suits with a center vent in the back, which tends to ride on the rear end rather than fall over it.

FOR WOMEN

1 Choose classic-fit trousers and tunic shirts and blouses.
Even if a bit tight, these garments will fit better and look more appropriate than severely cut items. Blouses can be worn untucked, but only if they are cut straight across the bottom and not high on the sides. If you carry extra weight in your hips, avoid narrow-leg pants; instead opt for classic or wide leg styles.

2 Use safety pins on pants with side and rear closures.
Safety pins can be used to extend the waistband and may even be used in a chain of two or three. Wear a long jacket or over-blouse to hide the pins; take care in windy conditions.

3 Pick structured garments.
Jackets and cardigan sweaters that have a structured shape—even without you in them—hide pounds. Look for jackets that have shoulder pads, back seams that curve, and tapered sleeves. Unlike the boxy suits men should wear, women's suits should be tapered, giving the appearance of a slimmer waistline.

4 Layer tops and use tops as shirt-jackets.
Blouses that are too tight when buttoned can be worn partially unbuttoned over a round-neck or turtleneck knit top. Leave the over-blouse unbuttoned down to a button above the waist; tuck the top and blouse into your skirt/pants for a slimming layered look. Add a jacket, or wear the blouse completely unbuttoned as a shirt-jacket if it is cut straight across the bottom.

how to fit into clothing that is too tight

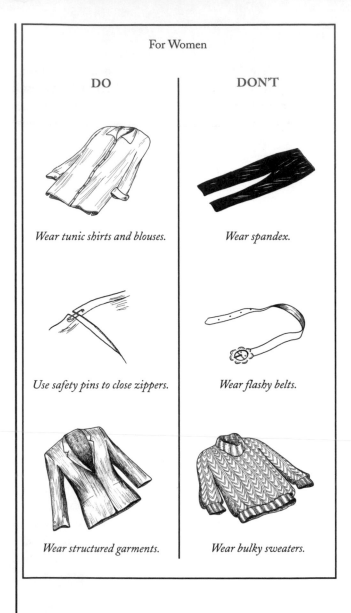

For Women

DO

Wear tunic shirts and blouses.

Use safety pins to close zippers.

Wear structured garments.

DON'T

Wear spandex.

Wear flashy belts.

Wear bulky sweaters.

5 Choose monochromatic ensembles.
Wear dark suits, or pair a black skirt or pants with a black top or blouse. To maximize the slimming effect of dark, monochromatic ensembles, keep the darkest garment on the bottom. Place lighter shades of the same hue near your face.

6 Wear bright colors properly.
To wear bright colors and still look thin, pair them with dark neutrals. Wear black pants/skirt with a brightly colored blouse or knit top, topped off with a black jacket. Or choose a red jacket with a black top and black pants/skirt.

7 Draw attention to the face with striking accessories, stylish hair, and tastefully applied makeup.

Be Aware

- Avoid clingy knits and spandex. These materials keep no secrets and tend to draw the eye to bulges. Lycra creates some stretch in a garment and is far more forgiving than spandex.
- Before the holidays, purchase a few blouses and two pairs of dark pants that are one size too big. Wear them before the holidays and people will think you've lost weight. After the holidays, they will fit perfectly.
- Avoid drawing attention to the waist with flashy belts over large shirts.

HOW TO SILENCE
A GROUP
OF CAROLERS

⭐ Turn out the lights.
As soon as you hear or see the carolers coming down the street, douse the lights. A dark house may deter them from stopping, since they will think no one is home. Turning out the lights belatedly—after they have arrived at your door—will send a strong message, but carolers are frequently very determined.

⭐ Turn up your music.
Without opening your door, play CDs at high volume. Speed metal and 1970s rock are likely to be in a different key than the carolers, who will be unable to stay in tune, become discouraged, and depart. If you are listening to Christmas music, shut it off immediately, or they may be encouraged to sing along.

⭐ Answer the door in a robe or towel.
Embarrassed, the carolers may simply leave. Nudity (even partial) may offend them and make them unable to sing. Call to another person inside the house (real or imaginary), "I'll be right back."

⭐ Answer the door holding a telephone.
Shout, "I can't hear you! There are carolers singing!" into the mouthpiece until the carolers move on.

chapter 3: holiday emergencies

Answer the doorbell partially dressed
in order to frighten off carolers.

★ Bribe them.
Tell them you would like to make a small donation, and that you enjoy their singing—from a distance.

★ Request songs they will not know.
The song repertoire of the caroler is generally quite shallow. Good choices to stump the carolers include "Adam Lay Ybounden," "Riu, Chiu," and "The Zither Carol."

★ Send them to someone else.
Smile and point to the house of a stranger or a neighbor you dislike, and say, "My friend over there really loves carols!" A house that is lavishly decorated for the season will prove irresistible to them.

HOW TO SING ALONG WHEN YOU DON'T KNOW THE WORDS

★ Request "Deck the Halls."
Every verse ends with "Fa La La La La, La La La La," which is easy to remember.

★ Just join in.
Carolers are irrepressible: If you are lost (or off-key), they will simply sing louder to drown you out.

★ Listen for the chorus.
Most carols have a repeating section, or chorus. Listen for it, and then sing only that part.

★ Lip-synch.
Move to the back of the group, then move your mouth soundlessly as they sing.

Be Aware

- Do not attempt to discourage carolers by stating that you are Jewish: You will get "Light the Menorah," "The Dreidel Song," "Sunrise, Sunset," or another menu of ethnic songs.
- Do not tell carolers that you don't celebrate Christmas: You are likely to hear "Frosty the Snowman," "Sleigh Ride," "Jingle Bell Rock," or a litany of secular holiday songs.
- Do not attempt to avoid carolers by going to the bathroom; they will be waiting when you return.

CHAPTER 4

SHOPPING SURVIVAL

HOW TO EVADE A STAMPEDE OF SHOPPERS

★ Stay focused and visualize your goal.
Do not freeze in front of the pack; do not wait for the crowd of shoppers to get close before you make your move. Reacting early and decisively in crowds offers your best shot at survival.

Brace for an oncoming crowd by wrapping your arms tightly around your packages.

⭐ Avoid herd mentality.

Animals travel in herds because there is safety in numbers, and the safest place is at the center of the pack, insulated from predators. Avoid the temptation to join the herd—you cannot shop if you cannot see the merchandise.

⭐ Do not move toward the oncoming herd.

You risk being trampled if you try to thread your way through a stampede. If you are unable to get out of the way of a fast-moving crowd, bring your arms in tightly around any packages you are carrying, turn your body in the direction of the crowd, and let yourself be carried along as you work your way to the outside of the herd.

⭐ Maximize your movement options.

If you need to negotiate a crowd, stay on the edge. Use the space near the walls to gain a few extra yards of room. Most shoppers will leave at least several feet between themselves and surrounding walls. This will give you room to maneuver.

Be Aware

When heading into a shopping situation where crowds may be present, wear proper shoes. Open-toed shoes offer minimal protection for your feet, and high heels will restrict your mobility. Select shoes with flat heels. Rubber soles provide better traction.

how to evade a stampede of shoppers

How to Penetrate a Crowd to Get the Last Item on the Shelf

1 Move slowly and decisively toward the front without appearing too aggressive.
Shoving or cutting people off will provoke flying elbows and closed ranks.

2 Keep your eyes on the other shoppers, so you can anticipate their movements.

3 Maintain a calm demeanor as you close in on the target item.
Breathe evenly and slowly. Avoid signaling your urgency, which might alert the crowd to the desirability of the toy or other target. Avoid stepping on toes or panicking other shoppers, which may cause a stampede.

4 Smile.

5 Grab the item.
Tuck it under your arm as you would a football to prevent it from being knocked or torn loose.

6 Proceed to the nearest cash register.
Continue to move with the crowd until you are able to slip down an aisle unnoticed.

HOW TO DEAL WITH A BAD GIFT

⭐ **Do not lie.**
If you receive a gift you simply detest, do not complicate the situation by lying. Do not praise the gift and say that you've always wanted one: The giver may later wonder why you are not using the gift or why it is not displayed in your home—or you may get something similar next year. If you receive an awful sweater, say something neutral like, "I love sweaters." If the giver is still not convinced that you like the present, try it on; you may also be able to offer another partially true compliment: "What a perfect fit!" If you receive as a gift something you already own, you do not need to advise the giver. Say, "I love this [thing]. How did you know?"

⭐ **Thank the giver for the thought, not the gift.**
Say, "How thoughtful of you" or "Thanks for thinking of me" or "I can't tell you how much this means to me."

⭐ **Do not overpraise the gift or the giver.**
Keep your thanks simple and brief.

⭐ **Determine where the gift was purchased.**
If there was no gift receipt, check the packaging, label, and tags for a store name. If you cannot determine where it was purchased, ask the giver appreciatively: "Where did you ever find this?" Note the name in order to return the gift later.

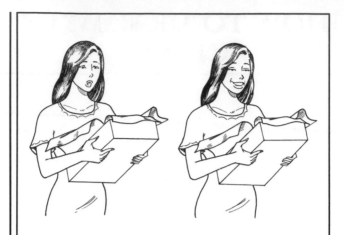

Do not show shock or disappointment when presented with a bad gift. Smile: Remember, it's the thought that counts.

✪ Regift it.
Unwrap the gift completely to make certain that it does not contain a hidden card, monogramming, or other giver- or recipient-specific identification. Rewrap it in fresh wrapping materials.

Be Aware
Regifting can be risky. You may later be embarrassed if you do not know where the gift you gave was purchased. Some regifts, particularly distinctive ones, may make the rounds (see "How to Repurpose a Fruitcake," page 26) and end up being regifted to the original giver, a situation you may find hard to explain.

chapter 4: shopping survival

HOW TO THWART GIFT SNOOPERS

⭐ Wrap gifts immediately.
Snoopers will begin searching long before the holidays. Wrap gifts as soon as you bring them home to avoid early detection.

⭐ Add items to the package.
Include marbles, bells, silverware, small weights, or paper clips in the box before wrapping. These will throw off shakers.

⭐ Switch the name tags.
Put the wrong name tags on gifts to confuse and frustrate snoopers.

Adding objects such as bells, marbles, or silverware
before wrapping will confuse snoopers.

★ Move gifts frequently.
Snoopers will check a hiding spot and then move on. Changing the location of gifts will lessen the chance they will be found.

★ Use a box significantly larger than the gift.
Good snoopers will be attuned to the sizes of specific gifts. Use larger-than-necessary boxes to throw them off the trail, and stiff cardboard to thwart squeezers.

★ Use multiple boxes.
Put the gift in a series of wrapped boxes, one inside the other, to frustrate the snooper and deter even the most persistent opener. Use glue instead of tape to secure wrapping paper, since glue is more likely to cause the paper to rip, deterring a rewrapper from proceeding further.

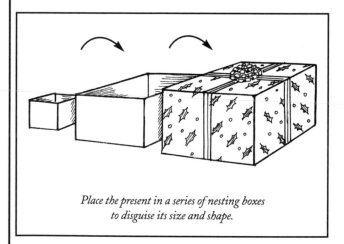

Place the present in a series of nesting boxes to disguise its size and shape.

Switching the name tags on gifts will throw off snoopers.
Remember to switch them back before the presents are opened.

✪ Wrap a fake present.
Box, wrap, and tag an old shoe, broken video cassette, or used tennis balls. A snooper who discovers and opens this "gift" will be flummoxed and suitably punished; he may be outraged at the pathetic present, but will be unable to say anything without giving himself away.

Be Aware
Keep track of your protective and evasive measures. If you've scrambled name tags, you will need to know who is really to receive each present. If you've added items to the box or used boxes within boxes, you will need to explain their presence to their recipients. If you added silverware, you may want to remove it before delivering the gift, lest you never see your silver again. If you've moved the presents too many times, you may forget where you placed them. Try to avoid having to rewrap all the presents at the last minute to undo your thwarting devices.

HOW TO DETERMINE THE CONTENTS OF A WRAPPED GIFT

WITHOUT OPENING THE PRESENT

1 Observe the position of the gift.
If the box is on top of a stack of gifts or hidden on a high shelf, it is probably not fragile. If it seems to have been carefully stored, use caution when handling.

2 Note the gift's surroundings.
Draw a quick diagram or take a digital or instant-developing photo that shows the location of the gift relative to other presents or objects around it. You will need to return the gift to exactly the same location and position later.

3 Examine the wrapping paper.
The name of the store may be printed on the paper, or it may be sealed using a sticker from the store. Both will give clues to its contents.

4 Smell the box.
Chocolates, baked goods, bath products, and leather goods have distinctive aromas, as do many other items.

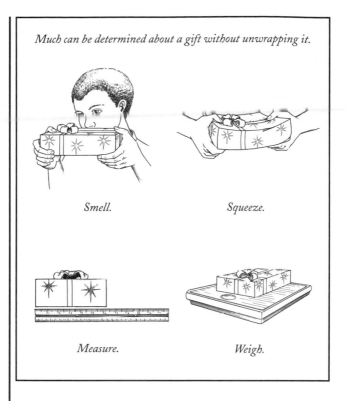

Much can be determined about a gift without unwrapping it.

Smell.

Squeeze.

Measure.

Weigh.

5 Squeeze the package.

Clothing boxes are generally light and will give slightly when squeezed. Electronics and other fragile items are usually packed in molded foam inserts that fit snugly inside thin outer boxes. Power tools are often packaged in rigid, thick cardboard boxes with large staples in the end flaps; you might be able to feel the staples through wrapping paper.

6 Measure the package.
Clothing boxes are generally longer than they are wide, and less than six inches high. Compact disc jewel cases are $5^1/_2$ inches wide, $4^3/_4$ inches long, and less than $^1/_2$ inch high. If the package has the first two dimensions but is higher (thicker), it is probably several discs or a double- or triple-disc set. DVD boxes are $5^1/_2$ inches wide, about $7^1/_2$ inches long, and $^1/_2$ inch high. Books may be any form of rectangle but are relatively heavy for their size. Underwear and socks will often be wrapped but not boxed; the packages will be flexible, and the plastic may make a quiet, crinkling sound.

7 Shake the package gently.
If you hear slight rustling, the item is likely clothes covered in tissue paper. If the box is big, heavy, and clinks slightly, it may contain an appliance.

8 Weigh the package.
If you have a hunch about the item and the store it came from, go online and compare the weight of the box to the listed shipping weight of the suspected gift.

How to Rewrap a Gift

You will need the original wrapping paper, still taped but with the tape slit where it crosses edges; a roll of clear tape (or that which matches the tape on the gifts); glue; a ruler; and, in emergencies, a roll of wrapping paper that matches as closely as possible the pattern of the original wrapping paper.

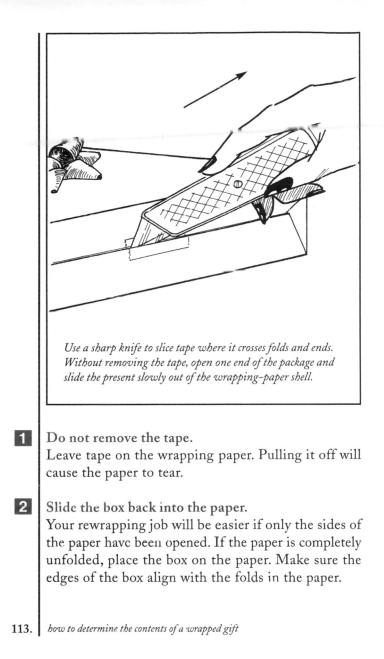

Use a sharp knife to slice tape where it crosses folds and ends. Without removing the tape, open one end of the package and slide the present slowly out of the wrapping-paper shell.

1 Do not remove the tape.
Leave tape on the wrapping paper. Pulling it off will cause the paper to tear.

2 Slide the box back into the paper.
Your rewrapping job will be easier if only the sides of the paper have been opened. If the paper is completely unfolded, place the box on the paper. Make sure the edges of the box align with the folds in the paper.

3 Follow the original wrapper's sequence.
Most wrappers will fold the paper around the gift first, then fold and seal the box at both ends. Follow the existing pattern of folds on the paper as you would in refolding a map. Use the ruler to re-crease the paper.

4 Glue or tape the paper.
If the opening was done properly, line up the old tape pieces and place glue under the flaps. This will give the tape a seamless appearance and avoid excess taping, which might be spotted. Hold the flaps of paper in place for several minutes until the glue sets. Wipe off any visible glue while it is still wet. If the opening was sloppy or the tape edges cannot be properly aligned, place a new, slightly larger piece over the old one.

5 Retie bows.
If the bows were hand-tied, retie them. If they were store-bought, make certain they are still stuck to the paper. If not, glue them on.

6 Reposition the gift.
Put the gift back in its original position. Refer to your diagram or photo (see "How to Determine the Contents of a Wrapped Gift," step 2, page 110).

7 Act surprised.
When you are given the present and open it legitimately, express delight. If the present you receive is not the one you opened and rewrapped, do not show surprise: The giver may have switched name tags (see "How to Thwart Gift Snoopers," page 107).

HOW TO WRAP A PRESENT WITHOUT WRAPPING PAPER

★ Use newspaper.
Newspapers (especially the colorful Sunday comics section) are a readily available substitute for wrapping paper. Avoid news sections that may have depressing headlines.

★ Use tissue paper.
Many stores provide tissue paper for packing the gift inside the box. Use that tissue to wrap the box.

★ Use brown paper bags.
Cut apart brown paper grocery bags; use them inside out if they are printed.

★ Use shopping bags.
Cut off the handles and bottoms and use the glossy shopping bags from the store. Some stores also put festive designs on their bags during the holiday season, giving your wrapping job a colorful touch.

★ Use aluminum foil.
Bright and shiny, foil is an excellent choice for giftwrap. Consider making small foil sculptures and putting them on top of the gift for added flair. Take care not to rip the foil, which tears easily. Alternatively, use waxed paper.

how to wrap a present without wrapping paper

★ Use shelf paper.
If you do not have a roll of shelf paper, remove the paper that lines your drawers. Carefully peel it off (it should come up easily), wipe with a damp cloth, and cut to fit the present.

★ Use colored plastic wrap.
Plastic wrap intended for food storage comes in several colors, including red and green. Use it to wrap gifts, then shrink to fit using a hair dryer.

★ Use fabric.
Any fabric or cloth can be used as giftwrap. Gather the fabric around and tie with yarn for a homey touch. It is not necessary to hem the fabric. If using clothing or socks, be sure they are clean.

★ Use sticky notes.
Multicolored sticky notes can make an attractive pattern or layered effect.

★ Use tissues.
Facial tissues, if applied carefully, can be a colorful, soft giftwrap. Use toilet paper only as a last resort.

HOW TO WRAP A PRESENT WITHOUT TAPE

★ Use ribbon, string, or yarn.
Fold the paper as tightly as possible, then wrap ribbon or other string around the box to hold everything together.

★ Use envelopes.
Cut the sticky strips from the flaps of envelopes, moisten, and use as you would tape.

★ Use stamps.
Use one-cent stamps, if available.

★ Make paste.
Mix half a cup of water and 1 cup flour. Stir while heating the mixture over a low flame. Allow the batter to cool and use as you would glue.

★ Use gum.
Regular chewing gum works best; bubble gum is not as adhesive. Chew each piece for two minutes. Apply sparingly.

how to wrap a present without wrapping paper

HOW TO TREAT A WRAPPING-PAPER CUT

1 Keep the victim calm and immobile.
A paper cut can cause intense pain at the injury site, but such cuts are usually superficial lacerations and rarely dangerous, except in the case of infection.

2 Instruct the victim to lie down if he/she feels faint.
After the initial rush of pain, the brain will become habituated to the discomfort and the pain will subside.

3 If the injury is to the finger, keep the finger straight.
Especially if the laceration crosses a knuckle, keep the finger straight to prevent pulling of the skin, which will increase pain. Hold the victim's other hand, if necessary.

4 Inspect the wound.
In the unlikely event that foreign material is lodged in the wound, remove the debris using sterilized tweezers.

5 Clean the wound.
Use warm water and soap to thoroughly wash out the wound.

6 Disinfect the injured area.
Treat the wound with isopropyl alcohol or hydrogen peroxide. This treatment may momentarily irritate the cut and cause slight pain.

7 Apply pressure.
Residual bleeding may occur if the cut is deep. Put pressure on the injury site, using a sterile bandage or clean cloth.

8 Treat with an antibiotic ointment.
Apply a topical antibiotic to impede bacterial growth.

9 Dress the wound.
Use a sterile bandage or adhesive strip. Until the wound heals, avoid contact with lemon juice and salt at the site of the wound: Both will cause intense pain.

10 Take pain medication, if necessary.
An especially deep paper cut may cause prolonged pain, which can be treated with an over-the-counter pain reliever such as aspirin, acetaminophen, or ibuprofen. Aspirin can thin the blood and may cause the wound to ooze for a longer period of time, however.

Be Aware

- In rare cases, a serious paper cut may be very deep and create a large flap of torn skin. Such an injury may require a butterfly bandage or stitches. If the wound does not stop bleeding even after applying continual pressure, or if an infection develops, seek medical attention.
- Open presents slowly.

CHAPTER 5
SURVIVING THE GREAT OUTDOORS

HOW TO ESCAPE A RUNAWAY PARADE BALLOON

1 Watch for sudden changes in wind speed.
Parade balloons are only deployed if sustained winds are 23 mph or less, with gusts no more than 34 mph. If the winds exceed these levels during the parade, controlling the balloons becomes much more difficult. If you detect a significant change in wind speed or direction, look for other indications of danger.

2 Watch the anchor vehicles.
Large balloons (5,000 cubic feet and bigger) will be tethered to two anchor vehicles that look like over-sized golf carts. These vehicles weigh two and a half tons each and act as failsafes, keeping a balloon from moving uncontrollably in case of emergency. In calm winds, the vehicles will be directly under the balloon and in the center of the street. If the anchor vehicles begin to move outward, toward the sidewalks, the wind is increasing substantially.

3 Watch the height of the balloon.
In calm winds, balloons will float at a maximum height of 50 feet. If the balloons are lower than this, winds may be dangerously high. In very strong winds, balloons may be almost at ground level.

Signs of danger: anchor vehicles moving toward curb, handlers reigning in the ropes.

4 Observe balloon handlers.
Each balloon has at least one handler; the largest balloons may have 50. Each handler holds a rope, and each rope is marked in foot increments. As winds increase, handlers will pull in their ropes and move into the wind for better control of the balloon in a headwind. If you see handlers reining in lots of rope, they are dealing with a clear and present danger.

how to escape a runaway parade balloon

5 Do not try to rescue a balloon.
It is difficult for an observer to gauge the enormity of a parade balloon, the tension in the ropes, and the amount of energy required to control a balloon in high winds. Lending a helping hand may seem easy, but the situation may be more out of control than it looks. Stay clear of the street and the balloon operators. Balloons and their handlers need lots of space to maneuver. Never attempt to pull on any ropes, and do not poke or prod any balloon.

6 Avoid lampposts and traffic lights.
The most immediate risk is that a runaway balloon may knock over a traffic light or lamppost, which will strike those standing below. Often, traffic lights are either removed or repositioned before the parade; if any remain, stay away from them.

7 Do not panic.
A stampeding crowd is a greater threat than a renegade balloon. If you have detected the early signs of danger and have responded, you will be moving ahead of the crowd.

8 Evacuate the area.
Seek safety away from the parade route, if you have time. You may take immediate shelter in a building or subway station.

HOW TO DEAL WITH A CANCELED FLIGHT

1 Do not stand in line.
When a flight is canceled, for any reason, hundreds of people line up at the ticket counter for rebooking. Ignore them and find a telephone.

Do not stand in line at the ticket counter. Locate a telephone and call the airline to book a new flight.

2 | Call the airline.
Ask the airline (or your travel agent) for a seat on the next flight going to your destination. You will get into the airline's computer system quickly, without having to stand in line. Your airline may be able to transfer your ticket to another flight on that airline, in which case you can proceed directly to the gate.

3 | Book a new flight.
Carry a list of all airlines that fly to your destination. The airline on which you are ticketed may not be able to rebook you on a later flight, or might not be the airline with the next available flight. Call other airlines and book a seat on a convenient flight. Depending on the fare you originally purchased and its restrictions, it might be simpler and faster to purchase a new ticket on a different airline, over the phone, and not use your original ticket. If you purchase a new ticket, proceed directly to the new airline's gate.

4 | Have your ticket endorsed.
If you have made a reservation on a different airline but have not purchased a new ticket, you will need to get your existing ticket endorsed over to the new carrier. You will have to stand in line at the counter of the airline that canceled the flight, but you, unlike others in line, will already have another flight arranged.

5 | Save unused tickets.
Unused tickets, one-way or round-trip, are almost as good as cash: They can be credited toward another flight on the same airline or, in some cases, refunded.

Be Aware

- When flying within the United States, know Rule 240, which covers what an airline will do for you in the event of a flight delay or cancellation. Legally, airlines must compensate only ticketed passengers who arrive on time but are denied a seat. In the event of a lengthy flight delay or cancellation, airlines as a matter of good public relations generally will provide passengers a hotel, meal, free phone call, and other amenities (be sure to ask if they're not offered) or arrange flights on another airline. Check each airline's website for their delay/cancellation policies.

- If you know you will be traveling on a busy holiday weekend to a very busy airport, and especially if there is the possibility of severe weather, book a room in an airport hotel; you will be ready if your flight is canceled. Check the hotel's cancellation policy, so you are not charged for an unused room, and be sure to cancel the room if you don't need it.

- Do not use electronic tickets if there is a chance of bad weather, labor problems, or security delays. The computer systems of different airlines cannot communicate with one another, so e-tickets cannot be endorsed from one airline to another. A paper ticket must first be issued, extending the amount of time you will have to spend at the ticket counter.

- Carry on your bags whenever possible. If your luggage has been checked through to your final destination but you encounter delays, you may not be able to switch your luggage's flights and airlines as easily as your own.

how to deal with a canceled flight

HOW TO DRIVE IN A BLIZZARD

1 Keep windows clear.
Use the heater, wipers, and defroster to keep windows clear and free of condensation. Do not let the car get too warm, however—the heat may put you to sleep.

2 At night, use low-beam headlights.
High-beams will reflect off the snow, making it more difficult to see.

3 Drive in high gear.
Do not downshift. Use as high a gear as possible for maximum traction and to avoid skids on snowy and icy roads.

4 Drive slowly.
Do not drive at maximum speed. Drive at a slow, constant speed.

5 Avoid sudden movements.
Do not brake, change gears, or accelerate around turns. Slow down and move into a lower gear approaching the turn, then simply steer around the bend.

6 Watch for ice.
Slow down before you reach icy or snowy patches of roadway. Skids are much more likely to occur on ice than on snow.

IF YOU SKID

1 Undo your last action.
Take your foot off the brake, or ease off the accelerator, depending upon whether you attempted to slow down or to speed up.

2 Steer into the skid.
To straighten the wheels, turn the steering wheel in the direction the car is moving. Do not jerk the wheel: steer smoothly to avoid further skidding. You may have to turn the wheel in one direction, then the other, to regain control and move straight.

3 Pump the brake pedal to slow down.
If the brakes are anti-lock, simply depress the brake pedal, and your car will automatically pump the brakes.

4 Check for traffic.
If you have come to a stop, or if you have spun out of your lane or slowed more than other traffic, you need to be especially careful not to block other vehicles.

IF YOU GET STUCK IN THE SNOW

1 Turn your wheels from side to side a few times to push snow out of the way.

2 Place a traction aid under the drive wheels.
Possible objects include a floormat, bag of kitty litter, wood planks, cardboard, a blanket, or clothing.

While driver rocks the car back and forth, time your push to increase forward momentum.

3 Move passengers above the drive wheels.
Depending upon whether you have front-wheel or rear-wheel drive, move your passengers and heavy luggage to the front or rear of the passenger compartment. Increased weight over the drive wheels will help to gain traction.

4 Rock the car back and forth.
In a low gear, apply light pressure on the gas pedal to move as far forward as you can go without spinning, then release the pedal (or put in the clutch) so you roll back. Gradually, the car will move forward a few more inches with each back-and-forth rock and may gain enough momentum to roll out of its rut and gain traction.

5 Push the car.
If the car is still stuck, instruct passengers to push the car forward. Try rocking the car back and forth, with a well-timed push at the forward point.

If You Become Stranded

1 Stay with or in the car.
You can survive for several days in your car, especially if you have food and water and enough fuel to periodically run the engine and heater.

2 Clear the vents.
The vents for the heater are usually below the windshield wipers on the hood. The exhaust pipe is located under the rear bumper. A clear exhaust pipe allows you to run the engine without danger of carbon monoxide poisoning.

3 Open a window occasionally.
You will benefit from the fresh air, and will ensure that the windows do not become frozen shut.

4 If the car becomes completely buried, poke a breathing hole in the snow above the car.
Use an ice scraper or tire iron.

5 Light a candle inside the car.
If you do not smell any gas fumes, light a candle to provide extra warmth. The candle will also serve as a warning sign of carbon monoxide fumes; if the candle begins to flicker and die, ventilate the car quickly.

6 Put on extra clothing.
To conserve fuel, do not run the engine and heater at full blast. If you do not have enough extra clothing, use newspapers, seat covers, and maps. Huddle with passengers for warmth.

7 Watch for help.
If you have passengers, take turns sleeping so that someone is always alert for possible rescuers. Use a portable radio for news updates; to conserve fuel or your car battery, do not use the car radio.

8 Ration food and drink.
Open and use any useful holiday presents you may be carrying, whether clothing, equipment, food, or beverages. Avoid alcohol, which feels warming but actually lowers your body temperature.

Be Aware
Prepare for a drive in potentially snowy conditions by packing smart. Take extra clothing (including gloves and a water-resistant jacket), blankets and pillows, boots, food and drink, a battery-operated radio and flashlight, matches and candles, a mobile phone, and several wooden planks (or a bag of kitty litter) for traction. Also take a shovel, if possible.

HOW TO STOP A RUNAWAY ONE-HORSE OPEN SLEIGH

1 Stay in the sleigh.

Grip the seat or railing with one hand and the reins with the other. Most injuries occur when the rider is thrown, falls, or jumps off the sleigh, hitting the ground or a tree or rock. If you cannot reach the reins or they are loose and dragging on the ground, do not attempt to reach them. Hold onto the sleigh and wait for the horse or horses to tire.

2 Tug and release the reins with a medium pressure. Repeat until the horse begins to slow down.

Hold on.

3 | Do not jerk the reins of a horse that is running at full speed.

Never pull a running horse off balance, which might cause it to stumble or fall. Horses can run at a speed of 25 to 30 miles per hour while pulling a sleigh.

4 | When the horse slows to a lope or a trot, pull one rein to the side.

With steady pressure, move the horse's head all the way around toward you. This will cause the horse to begin going in a circle. The horse will quickly tire of circling, begin to feel that you are in control again, and slow to a walk.

5 | Pull back with slow, steady pressure on both reins until the horse stops.

Once the horse is at a walk, it is safe to bring it to a complete stop.

6 | Dismount.

Be Aware

If a runaway sleigh is coming toward you, do not attempt to grab the horse or the reins. Even if you could grab a rein, that would more likely result in a broken rein than a stopped horse. Let the driver have space to gain control. Standing in front of a runaway horse and flapping your arms will not cause the horse to stop.

How to Jump from a Runaway Sleigh

Abandoning the sleigh should be a last resort. If the sleigh is headed for imminent peril, however, you will need to jump.

1 Move to the edge of the sleigh.
Remain seated until the last moment, holding on to the seat or railing.

2 Stuff your clothing with blankets or seat cushions to reduce the impact.
Give yourself as much protective padding as is readily available.

3 Open the sleigh door, if there is one.

4 Pick your landing spot.
If you can, wait until the horse rounds a bend, since it may slow down. The ideal landing spot will be well covered with soft snow and free of trees, rocks, and bushes.

5 Crouch low to the floor of the sleigh.
Bend your knees.

6 Jump perpendicular to the sleigh.
Leaping at a right angle away from the sleigh will make it much less likely for you to fall under the runners. Leap as far away as you can.

7 | Cover your head.
Use your hands and arms to protect your head.

8 | Land flat.
Do not attempt to land on your feet or do a somer-sault. Keep your body straight and try to land so that all parts of your body hit the ground at the same time. This will spread the impact over a wider area.

9 | Roll like a log.

If headed for imminent peril, jump perpendicular to the sleigh, land flat, and roll like a log.

HOW TO FEND OFF A CHARGING REINDEER

1 Stand your ground.
Most reindeer have been bred to be docile livestock;
they are sometimes referred to as "tundra cows." They
will run around, rather than over, a standing person,
even when charging in a herd.

2 Watch for reindeer in rut.
Reindeer mate from late August to October, when
they will be in rut, or heat, and much more dangerous. Each male, or bull, will keep a harem of females
and will become unpredictable and aggressive with
any person who approaches. While both male and
female reindeer have antlers, male reindeer are noticeably larger, weighing 400 pounds or more. During
rut, necks on males will be large and swollen.

3 Watch for front-leg kicking.
When disturbed, reindeer will rear up on the hind
legs and kick out with the front hooves. Females are
generally not dangerous except when defending
calves. Stay well back and to the side to avoid being
kicked. During rut, reindeer bulls will try to gore
rather than kick, if antagonized.

Stand your ground. Grab the reindeer by the antlers and direct its charge away from you.

4 Watch for antler display.
Before goring, a male will often attempt to intimidate by showing, or "presenting," its antlers, turning his head to the side. Be wary in approaching or cornering a bull reindeer during this display.

5 Back up slowly.
Speak to the reindeer in a soft voice. Do not make any sudden movements.

6 Do not raise your arms over your head.
The bull may take this as a challenge sign that you are also displaying antlers.

7 | If the reindeer attempts to gore you, grab the antlers.
Grasp one branch with each hand and attempt to steer the head away from you. If the reindeer tries to lunge forward, you may not be able to stop it, but guiding the antlers may allow you to redirect its charge.

8 | Move to the side quickly as you release the antlers.
The reindeer will now be beside you and may just move away. Do not run, or you will call attention to yourself. Carefully put distance between yourself and the reindeer.

9 | Call for help.
Using a voice and tone that does not further antagonize the reindeer, advise others in the area of your situation. They may be able to distract the reindeer, if it is still in pursuit.

Be Aware

- Caribou, which are much more aggressive and dangerous, are often mistaken for reindeer. Reindeer have shorter legs and are rounder.
- Male reindeer have huge antlers, with as many as 14 to 18 points per side.

HOW TO RESCUE SOMEONE STUCK IN A CHIMNEY

1 Obtain a long, sturdy rope.
Make sure the rope is longer than the length of the chimney. You will need approximately 10 feet of rope for each story (including the attic), plus 10 additional feet.

2 Tie a knot in the rope every two feet.

3 Position yourself on the roof of the house.
The opening of the chimney at the fireplace end is probably too narrow for you to pull the person out. You must perform your rescue from above.

4 Communicate with the person.
Make sure that the person who is stuck is still conscious and able to help with the rescue. Tell him you are coming.

5 Lower the rope down the chimney.
The rope should be tied securely around the chimney or another immovable object. Slowly feed the other end hand-over-hand down the chimney.

6 Tell the victim to grab the rope.
Holding onto the knots provides both you and the victim a better grip.

7 Pull the victim up.

Unless you are much larger than the victim (and very strong), you will not be able to pull the victim out unaided. The victim can help by using footholds to brace and climb. If the victim cannot climb out or otherwise help in the rescue, enlist others to help you pull the rope.

8 Call the fire department.

If you cannot extricate the person from the chimney, call the fire department for assistance.

HOW TO CLIMB DOWN A CHIMNEY

1 Feel and smell for a lighted fire.

Do not enter a chimney that is hot or smoking.

2 Assess the size and type of chimney.

Some chimney flues may be as narrow as 12 by 12 inches, too small for an adult to enter. Chimneys 24 by 24 inches or larger are ideal. Big, old houses are more likely to have large chimneys and less likely to have an entry-impeding damper at the bottom.

3 Remove the chimney cap.

Many chimney openings are covered with a cap to prevent animals from entering the flue. The cap will have either four short legs tucked into the chimney and held in place by gravity, or four pressure screws attached to the inside surface of the flue.

how to rescue someone stuck in a chimney

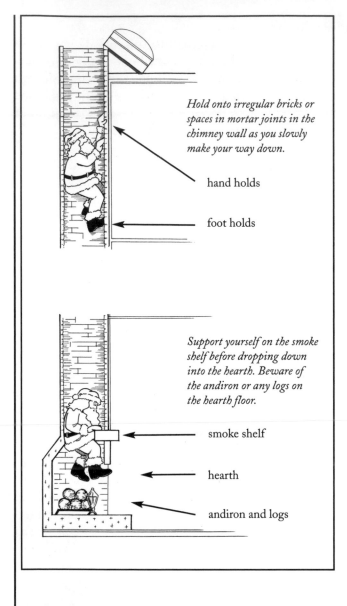

Hold onto irregular bricks or spaces in mortar joints in the chimney wall as you slowly make your way down.

hand holds

foot holds

Support yourself on the smoke shelf before dropping down into the hearth. Beware of the andiron or any logs on the hearth floor.

smoke shelf

hearth

andiron and logs

4 | Examine the inner surface of the chimney.
Use a flashlight to peer into the flue. Homes built after 1935 may have a flue lined with clay tiles. Older homes have unlined brick flues. Brick flues have a more irregular surface, offering better hand and footholds. Some newer homes may have metal-lined flues. Avoid these, as they offer minimal traction.

5 | Enter the chimney feet first.
Keep your hands above you and hold onto irregular bricks or spaces in the mortar joints. If the chimney is clay-lined, concentrate on the joints between the clay tiles for your handholds and footholds. These joints are two feet apart. The chimney is likely narrow enough that you can lean back against one wall while bracing your feet on the opposite wall.

6 | Move slowly toward the bottom of the chimney.
You will quickly be covered with creosote (hardened soot) unless the chimney has recently been cleaned. Fresh creosote may be powdery and difficult to grip, or sticky (formed by burning moist wood), aiding your descent. Old creosote will be hard, shiny, and very slick. Keep your body straight to lessen the chance of getting stuck on sticky soot.

7 | Look for the smoke chamber.
This brick-lined area is below the flue and has large amounts of soot and creosote. When you reach the smoke chamber, you will be just above the smoke shelf and close to the bottom of the chimney.

8 Use the smoke shelf to brace yourself.

The smoke shelf is a few feet above the hearth (the area where the fire is made, also called the "firebox"). This angled brick shelf is off to the bottom rear of the flue. It catches rain and funnels the wider area of smoke that comes from the hearth into the narrower passage of the flue. You may be able to rest your feet on it before continuing.

9 Open the damper.

Most fireplaces have a damper, a metal door that slides or swings closed to prevent drafts and to keep heat from escaping up the flue when no fire is present. Open the damper by pulling it toward you; use a heavy magnet if you cannot pull it open by hand. Some dampers use a screw-type mechanism that can be opened only from inside the house: If it or the damper is too small to pass through, or is screwed shut, you will have to climb back out the top of the chimney.

10 Lower yourself into the hearth.

If you can see the hearth, and can fit through the opening, carefully drop down into the fireplace and enter the house. Beware of an andiron or logs on the hearth floor.

HOW TO SURVIVE
A RUNAWAY SLED

1 Quickly survey the topography.
If you are sledding in a wide-open field with few
obstacles and no danger of a precipice, stay on the
sled and ride it out. The sled will eventually stop once
you reach level ground.

2 Slow the sled using emergency steering and braking.
Steer the sled side to side to slow it down. Drag your
feet (if feet first) or hands and feet (if head first) to
slow the sled or to steer.

3 Redirect the sled.
Turn the sled onto a course that traverses the hill, if
possible. Gradually try to turn uphill to lose speed.
An abrupt turn could send you flipping out of control.

4 Roll off the sled.
Perform a single, sideways roll off the sled. If you
were on your stomach, you will now be on your back
sliding head-first down the hill. Roll one more time
so that you are on your stomach. If you were riding
the sled feet-first, you will be on your stomach sliding
feet-first down the hill.

5 Protect, then roll.
If tumbling out of control on a hill with obstacles,
protect your head and face.

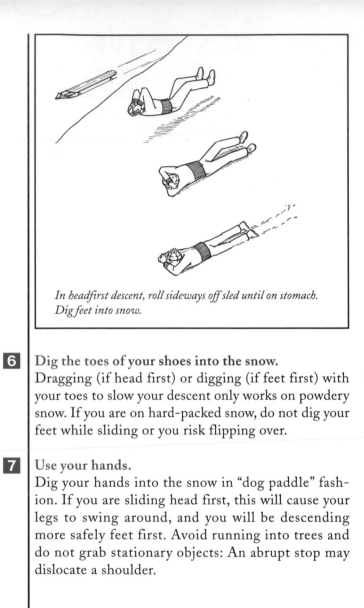

In headfirst descent, roll sideways off sled until on stomach. Dig feet into snow.

6 | Dig the toes of your shoes into the snow.
Dragging (if head first) or digging (if feet first) with your toes to slow your descent only works on powdery snow. If you are on hard-packed snow, do not dig your feet while sliding or you risk flipping over.

7 | Use your hands.
Dig your hands into the snow in "dog paddle" fashion. If you are sliding head first, this will cause your legs to swing around, and you will be descending more safely feet first. Avoid running into trees and do not grab stationary objects: An abrupt stop may dislocate a shoulder.

8 | Once stopped, push up from the side of the hill.
Get up by moving your weight to your hands and feet.
(Synthetic clothing slides on snow and tends to make
the body function as a sled.)

9 | Climb or descend the hill slowly or wait for help.
Do not remain in the middle of a hill being used by
sledders unless you are unable to move. Retrieve your
sled only if you can proceed safely.

Be Aware

If multiple riders have to abandon the sled, dive off
the sled on opposite sides, at staggered intervals, so
that you do not injure each other when you roll.

HOW TO WIN A SNOWBALL FIGHT

1 **Test the snow.**
Stick a twig, chopstick, or a thin utensil in the snow and pull it out quickly to determine the packing consistency. It should go in and come out smoothly, not hitting icy or solid patches. Snowball snow should not be frozen, nor should it be too dry ("powder") or too wet ("granular" or "corn"). The snow needs just enough moisture to hold together as you shape it.

2 **Doctor the snow.**
The best air temperature for snowball making is above 5° F and below 32° F. If the air temperature is below 5° F, warm the snow in your hands before attempting to make a snowball.

Have one person make fresh snowballs while another keeps an eye on the enemy.

3 | Establish a base camp.
Find a suitable location with good sight lines and plenty of fresh snow (see "How to Build a Snow Fort," page 151). Consider keeping a wall at your back to thwart flanking maneuvers.

4 | Begin preparations.
Make as many snowballs as you can in advance of the battle. A good snowball should be larger than a golf ball but smaller than a cantaloupe, and should hold its shape when others are stacked on top of it.

5 | Build a snowball sled.
Secure a wooden produce crate or waxed cardboard box to a sled's rope. Fill the box with snowballs. Use the snowball sled to transport ammunition or a fresh supply of snow.

6 | Use shields.
Maintain a supply of garbage can lids with handles; use these for shields during battle.

7 | Aim low and throw straight.
Snowball fight rules dictate that hitting in the face is forbidden. Aim for the chest or lower body. Ice balls or snowballs containing foreign material are also considered unfair.

8 | Secure prisoners.
Snowball fight rules provide for the taking of prisoners: An enemy hit three times is considered captured.

Captives may not be forced to fight their comrades, but may be pressed into service as snowball makers.

How to Make Snowballs

1 Scoop up two handfuls of snow.

2 Press your hands together around the snow to create a sphere.

3 Squeeze and rotate the sphere.
Add snow or take some away, squeeze, and rotate, until the ball is perfectly round. A smooth, perfectly rounded ball is more aerodynamic and will throw better. Make sure it is easy to pick up and throw.

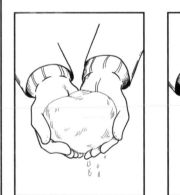

Scoop up two handfuls of snow, then squeeze and rotate until the ball is perfectly round.

4 Make more snowballs.
Good snowballs made from the right consistency snow will stack easily and not stick together. Keep a pile within arm's reach.

HOW TO BUILD A SNOW FORT

A Snow-Mound Fort

1 Find a pile of freshly plowed snow.
Snow plows create huge mounds of snow, saving you the trouble of creating one. Look in parking lots or on street corners for such piles. The pile should be at least four feet tall and several feet wide at the base. You will build your fort into this mound. Do not pick a mound on an active street that is likely to be replowed.

2 Compress the snow.
If you can find a big piece of plywood—about the size of a door—place it on top of the mound and use it to compress the snow until the mound is about four feet high. If you cannot locate plywood, lie down on the mound. Use good packing snow (see "How to Win a Snowball Fight," step 1, page 148).

3 Dig into the back of the mound.
Create a small entrance hole, strategically placed so the enemy cannot see or attack it easily.

4 | **Hollow out the mound.**
Dig out the center of the mound, pushing the snow out of the entrance hole. Use this snow for making snowballs.

5 | **Make peepholes.**
Punch through the wall opposite the entrance with your fist or the handle of a shovel every several feet to create observation holes. These will enable you to detect a surprise attack.

6 | **Defend your fort.**
A fort that is overrun can be used by your enemies.

A Block Fort

1 | **Find a wooden produce crate or waxed cardboard box.**
The box should be no larger than $1^1/_2$ by 2 feet. Remove the flaps, if any, from the top. Utilize several boxes and people to expedite the process.

2 | **Pack the box with snow.**
Pack tightly, with as little air as possible.

3 | **Remove the snow block.**
Turn the box over. Gently pull the sides of the box or tap the sides of the box until the block slides out.

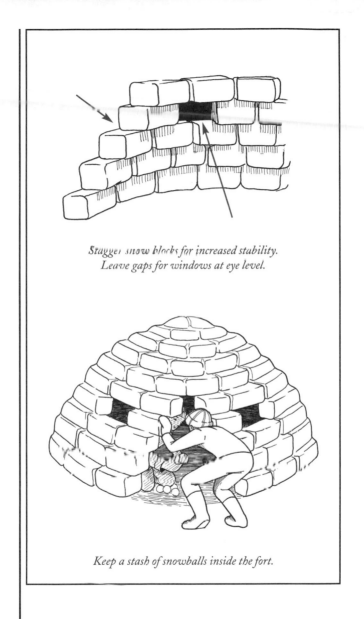

Stagger snow blocks for increased stability.
Leave gaps for windows at eye level.

Keep a stash of snowballs inside the fort.

4 | Amass snow blocks.
Repeat steps 2 and 3 until you have several dozen snow blocks.

5 | Build an igloo-shaped structure.
Place the bottom level of blocks in a circle 6 to 8 feet in diameter. Leave an open spot for the door. Stack the next layer on top, offsetting the ends in the traditional bricklaying pattern, and moving each block in a few inches toward the center. On either side of the door opening, move the blocks toward each other by a few inches, to make a roughly triangular opening. Repeat until the blocks meet at the top and there is enough room for you to crawl in. (You may need to trim blocks before placing them at the very top of the fort.) Omit a few blocks at eye level for windows.

6 | Fill in the cracks.
Use snow to fill in the spaces between the blocks.

7 | Reinforce.
Sprinkle the fort with water from a watering can and let the fort set overnight. In the morning it will be a hardened bastion.

Be Aware

• You may not always have time to get inside your fort when attacked. A good snow fort should be high enough to protect you from incoming snowballs if you hide behind it, but it should also be low enough for you to see around and throw over.

- Keep a stash of snowballs inside the fort.
- In case of a long, sustained siege, keep drinks, food, and blankets in the fort. Set them in a corner, out of the way of the action.
- Divide your manpower so there are scouts and hurlers outside, and snowball makers inside.

HOW TO TREAT A TONGUE STUCK TO A POLE

1 Do not panic.

2 Do not pull the tongue from the pole.
Pulling sharply will be very painful.

3 Move closer to the pole.
Get as close as possible without letting more of the tongue's surface area touch the pole.

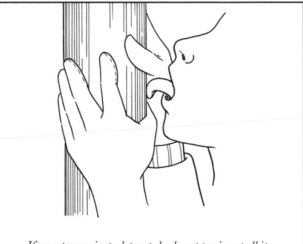

If your tongue is stuck to a pole, do not panic or pull it.
Warm the pole with your hands until your tongue comes loose.

4 | **Warm the pole with your hands.**
A tongue will stick when the surface of the pole is very cold. The top few layers of the tongue will freeze when the tongue touches the pole, causing bonding. Place your gloved hands on the area of the pole closest to the tongue. Hold them there for several minutes.

5 | **Take a test pull.**
As the pole warms, the frozen area around the tongue should begin to thaw. Gently pull the tongue away from the pole. You may leave a layer or two of skin on the pole, which will be painful, but the tongue will quickly heal.

Alternative Method

Use warm water.
Pour water from a water bottle over the tongue and the pole. Do not use water that is cold, or it may freeze and exacerbate the problem.

Be Aware

- Do not try to loosen your tongue with your own saliva. Although saliva is relatively warm, the small amount you will be able to generate is likely to freeze on your tongue.
- If another person is present, have him or her pour warm (not hot) water over your tongue. This may be difficult to articulate while your tongue is stuck—pantomiming a glass of water poured over your tongue should do the trick.

APPENDIX

THE "THERE IS NO SANTA CLAUS" SPEECH

Son/Daughter,

Please sit down over here by me. There's something I've been meaning to tell you for a long time, and I think you're old enough now.

I know you believe with all your heart that there is a person called Santa Claus who brings you presents every year if you are good. But the truth is that there is no Santa Claus. "Santa Claus" is really all the parents in the world, who love their children very much and buy them presents to show how much they love them.

Your presents are not made by elves in a toy shop at the North Pole. There is no such thing as an elf; and the North Pole is actually one of the loneliest and most desolate places on Earth. The truth is that mom and dad buy all your presents at the mall, and we're the ones who eat Santa's cookies and drink Santa's milk. Reindeer can't fly, either.

But don't cry. This doesn't mean that the spirit of Santa Claus isn't real. "Santa Claus" is inside all of us, whenever we give presents to those that we love or those who are less fortunate. When you grow up, you can be Santa, too. Or the Easter Bunny. Or the Tooth Fairy.

NEW YEAR'S RESOLUTION-O-MATIC

Choose one option from each of the concentric circles, beginning at the center, to create your New Year's resolutions.

THE EXPERTS

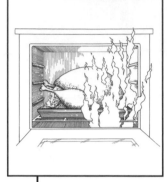

How to Extinguish a Burning Turkey

Source: *Recipe for Safer Cooking,* a publication of the Consumer Products Safety Commission.

How to Serve Burnt Turkey; How to Prevent a Turkey from Exploding; How to Keep a Turkey Moist During Cooking

Sources: David Burke is corporate chef for the Smith and Wollensky Restaurant Group, head chef at Park Avenue Café in New York City, and author of *Cooking with David Burke.* • Sherrie Rosenblatt is the director of public relations for the National Turkey Federation (www.eatturkey.com).

How to Remove a Gravy Stain

Sources: *Field Guide to Stains* by Virginia Friedman, Melissa Wagner, and Nancy Armstrong. • D. A. Burns & Sons is a Washington State–based carpet cleaning and textile craftsmanship company.

How to Put Out a Grease Fire

Sources: Meri-K Appy is vice president for public education at the nonprofit National Fire Protection Association (www.nfpa.org), which facilitates the development of national consensus safety codes and develops and implements public safety education and research initiatives. She oversees all of the NFPA's public education and community outreach programs. • Chris Miles is a lieutenant in the Philadelphia Fire Department.

How to Treat a Grease Burn
Source: Ken Zafren, M.D., is the medical director of Emergency Medical Services for the State of Alaska and a fellow of the American College of Emergency Physicians. He specializes in remote region and high-altitude trauma.

How to Repurpose a Fruitcake
Sources: Sarah Phillips is the author of *The Healthy Oven Baking Book* and the founder and president of Baking911.com. She is the creator of the Healthy Oven line of baking mixes and worked in food manufacturing for 10 years. • June Jacobs, a certified culinary professional, teaches cooking and wine classes. She leads food-and-wine focused tours of France through her company, Feastivals (www.feastivals.com), and is the author of *Feastivals Cooks at Home* and a director of the New York Association of Cooking Teachers. • Brother Barnabas Brownsey of the Cistercian Order of the Stritch Observance lives in Holy Cross Abbey and works in its Monastery Bakery in Berryville, Virginia (www.monasteryfruitcake.org).

How to Open a Bottle of Wine with a Broken Cork
Source: Daniel Dawson is the owner of Backroom Wines (www.backroomwines.com), a fine wine and wine tasting shop in Napa, California. He is a former sommelier at the French Laundry restaurant and a former wine merchant.

How to Avoid Shooting a Champagne Cork
Source: Daniel Dawson.

CHAPTER 2: FRIENDS AND FAMILY

How to Deal with a Meddling Parent
Source: Robin Thompson is the founder of the Etiquette Network (www.etiquette-network.com) and lectures on etiquette and image for all ages at schools, universities, and businesses. She is the author of *Be the Best You Can Be: A Guide to Etiquette and Self-Improvement for Children and Teens*.

How to Survive If You Have No One to Kiss on New Year's Eve
Source: Sherry Amatenstein (www.luvlessons.com) is the author of *The Q and A Dating Book: Answers to the Thorniest, Sexiest, Most Intimate and Revealing Questions About Love, Sex, and Romantic Relationships* and *Love Lessons from Bad Breakups: Discover How to Make Relationships Last—by Learning from the Ones That Didn't*, and is the dating columnist for ivillage.com.

How to Fend Off an Unwanted Kiss
Source: Sherry Amatenstein.

How to Overcome Holiday Depression
Source: Gerald H. Smith, D.D.S., is the author of the best-selling *Headaches Aren't Forever* and *Alternative Treatments for Conquering Chronic Pain*, and he maintains a clinical practice specializing in craniomandibular somatic disorders and pain therapy in Bucks County, Pennsylvania. He runs the International Center for Nutritional Research (www.icnr.com).

CHAPTER 3: HOLIDAY EMERGENCIES

How to Treat Food Poisoning
Source: Dave Hill is a UK–based food industry consultant who advises manufacturers and caterers on safe food production. He has written numerous guides to good hygiene practice and is a fellow of the Institute of Food Science and Technology (www.ifst.org).

How to Extinguish a Christmas Tree Fire
Sources: Meri-K Appy • Chris Miles.

How to Survive a Fall from a Ladder
Source: Ken Zafren

How to Survive Christmas Tree Light Disasters
Sources: Colin C. Adams, Ph.D., is the Francis C. Oakley Third Century Professor of Mathematics at Williams College. He is the author of *The Knot Book: An Elementary Introduction to the Mathematical Theory of Knots* and is the coauthor of *How to Ace Calculus: The Streetwise Guide.* • Michael Clendenin is executive director of Electrical Safety Foundation International (www.electrical-safety.org), a nonprofit dedicated to public awareness and education on electrical safety.

How to Resize a Christmas Tree
Source: Bill Asack owns and runs Asack and Son Tree Farm in Barton, Vermont (www.billasack.com).

How to Prevent a Tree from Toppling Over
Source: Bill Asack.

How to Treat Mistletoe Poisoning
Sources: Dan Brown, Ph.D., is an associate professor of Nutritional Toxicology at Cornell University and a staff scientist at the International Livestock Research Institute. • John P. Lamb, Pharm.D., CSPI, FCSHP, a toxicology management specialist and health educator for the Sacramento Division of the California Poison Control System (www.calpoison.org), is an assistant clinical professor of pharmacy at UCSF and an associate clinical professor of medicine at UCD. • Eric Lombardini, V.M.D., is a captain in the U.S. Army Veterinary Corps and the commander of a veterinary medical detachment responsible for care of military working dogs and other government-owned animals.

How to Make an Emergency Menorah
Source: Marsha Silver Heit is a Hebrew school teacher in Philadelphia

How to Make Menorah Candles from Crayons
Sources: Michelle Espino is the author of *Candlemaking for Fun and Profit* and is the owner of Waxed Out Candles (www.waxedout.com), an artisan studio in Tallahassee, Florida. • Amy Segelin owns Luminous Creations (www.luminouscreations.com), a maker and distributor of beeswax candles in Los Angeles.

How to Fit into Clothing That Is Too Tight
Source: Sherry Maysonave, author of *Casual Power: How to Power Up Your Nonverbal Communication and Dress Down for Success*, is the president and founder of Empowerment Enterprises (www.casualpower.com), a consulting firm specializing in communication and image.

How to Silence a Group of Carolers
Source: Kevin St. Clair is the director of Dickens and Company (www.dickensandcompany.com), a professional caroling group based in Southern California, which books carolers nationwide.

CHAPTER 4: SHOPPING SURVIVAL

How to Evade a Stampede of Shoppers
Sources: G. Keith Still, Ph.D., is a mathematician and crowd dynamics expert who runs workshops on crowds and crowd safety (www.crowddynamics.com). He is the

creator of the Legion system, a crowd modeling method used to assist in planning the Sydney Olympics. • Stevanne "Dr. Toy" Auerbach, Ph.D., is a child development specialist and the author of *Smart Play: How to Raise a Child with a High P.Q.* Her website, www.drtoy.com, provides year-round guidance on toys and play.

How to Deal with a Bad Gift
Source: Peter Post, great-grandson of Emily Post, is an expert in business and personal etiquette. He is author of *Etiquette Advantage in Business* and director of the Emily Post Institute (www.emilypost.com) in Burlington, Vermont.

How to Thwart Gift Snoopers
Sources: Sherri and Larry Athay are the authors of *Present Perfect: Unforgettable Gifts for Every Occasion* and the founders of Present Perfect Gift Consultants and GiftElan.com.

How to Determine the Contents of a Wrapped Gift
Sources: Sherri and Larry Athay.

How to Rewrap a Gift
Source: Juanita Lewis (www.itsawrapgifts.com) has been a professional gift-basket designer and wrapping specialist for 18 years. She teaches classes and produces instructional videos on bowmaking, gift baskets, and gift wrapping, and has served as a judge for 3M's annual "Most Gifted Wrapper" contest.

How to Wrap a Present Without Wrapping Paper
Source: Juanita Lewis.

How to Treat a Wrapping Paper Cut
Source: Seth Haplea, M.D., is a member of the American Academy of Neurology and the American Association of Electrodiagnostic Medicine. He practices clinical neurophysiology in Phoenix, Arizona.

Chapter 5: Surviving The Great Outdoors

How to Escape a Runaway Parade Balloon
Source: Henry Perahia is chief engineer for the New York City Department of Transportation and supervisor of the balloons for the Macy's Thanksgiving Day Parade in Manhattan.

How to Deal with a Canceled Flight
Source: Rudy Maxa is the publisher of a monthly consumer travel newsletter (www.rudymaxa.com). He is also a commentator on public radio's evening business show *Marketplace* and was the original host of public radio's weekend show *The Savvy Traveler*.

How to Drive in a Blizzard
Source: *The SAS Survival Driver's Handbook*, by John "Lofty" Wiseman.

How to Stop a Runaway One-Horse Open Sleigh

Sources: John and Kristy Milchick are horse trainers who own and manage Hideaway Stables (www.hideawayhorses.com), a horse farm in Kentucky, where they breed, train, and sell foundation American quarter horses. • Christopher Caso is a stuntman who has produced and performed high-fall stunts for numerous movies, including *Batman and Robin*, *The Lost World*, and *The Crow: City of Angels*.

How to Fend Off a Charging Reindeer

Source: Greg Finstad is program manager of the Reindeer Research Program of the University of Alaska, Fairbanks.

How to Rescue Someone Stuck in a Chimney

Sources: Karen Duke is one of only a few female certified chimney sweeps in the United States. She and her family operate Victorian Fireplace in Richmond, Virginia, which specializes in fireplaces for older homes. • Roger Hoelderlin runs Best Way Maintenance (www.bestwaychimney.com), a licensed and certified chimney sweep and masonry company based in Levittown, New York. • Craig Issod is the Webmaster of HearthNet (www.hearth.com).

How to Survive a Runaway Sled
Source: John Markel is the operator of Midnight Sun Locations (www.alaskafilmlocations.com), a film and television stunt, location, and safety consulting firm based in Girdwood, Alaska. He is certified in High Angle Rescue and has 30 years of rock and ice climbing experience.

How to Win a Snowball Fight; How to Make Snowballs

Sources: David and Jeanie Stiles (www.stilesdesigns.com) are the authors of *Treehouses, Huts, and Forts* and *Treehouses You Can Actually Build.* • Kenneth G. Libbrecht is a professor of physics and physics executive officer at Cal Tech, where he studies ice physics and crystal growth of ice.

How to Build a Snow Fort
Sources: David and Jeanie Stiles. • John Lindner, Director of the Wilderness Survival School for the Colorado Mountain Club, is also director of training for the Snow Operations Training Center, an organization that teaches mountain survival skills to utility companies, search and rescue teams, and government agencies.

How to Treat a Tongue Stuck to a Pole
Source: Kenneth G. Libbrecht.

ABOUT THE AUTHORS

David Borgenicht is a writer, editor, husband, and father who has survived dozens of holiday worst-case scenarios, from being trapped in a blizzard to potato latke disasters, caroling nightmares, and mistletoe mishaps. He lives in Philadelphia with his family, and knows who's naughty and nice.

Joshua Piven is a writer, editor, and fixture on the holiday circuit. He is the coauthor of *The Worst-Case Scenario Survival Handbook* series. He lives in Philadelphia with his wife.

Brenda Brown is a freelance illustrator and cartoonist whose work has been published in many books and major publications, including *The Worst-Case Scenario Survival Handbook* series, *Esquire*, *Reader's Digest*, *USA Weekend*, *21st Century Science and Technology*, the *Saturday Evening Post*, the *National Enquirer*, and many other magazines. Her work has also appeared in specialized education series, websites, and promotional ad campaigns. Brenda's website: http://webtoon.com.

Check out www.worstcasescenarios.com for updates, new scenarios, and more! Because you just never know . . .

ACKNOWLEDGMENTS

David Borgenicht extends his thanks and holiday wishes of good cheer to the following: Jay Schaefer, Steve Mockus, and Erin Slonaker for their tireless editing efforts; Terry for his fabulous holiday design work; all of our experts for their knowledge and, well, expertise; and Santa Claus, Hanukkah Harry, the Grinch, and the Heat Miser (for just being there).

Joshua "The Heat Miser" Piven thanks Rebecca and Karen Hafter for making the holidays fun and entertaining. He also thanks Linus for teaching Charlie Brown the true meaning of Christmas.

More Worst-Case Scenarios

The Worst-Case Scenario Survival Handbook

The Worst-Case Scenario Survival Handbook: Travel

The Worst-Case Scenario Survival Handbook: Dating & Sex

The Worst-Case Scenario Survival Handbook: Golf

The Worst-Case Scenario Survival Calendar

The Worst-Case Scenario Daily Survival Calendar

The Worst-Case Scenario Survival Journal

The Worst-Case Scenario Survival Cards: 30 Postcards

The Worst-Case Scenario Dating & Sex Address Book

The Worst-Case Scenario Holiday Survival Cards